Mental Maths Practice 5

Teacher's Book

Peter Clarke

Christina Rossiter

Heinemann

Introduction

Children need to develop mental strategies as all mathematical problems involve some form of mental activity. Pupils will be unable to complete practical investigations successfully unless they can hold mental images in their heads. To build these up and learn to manipulate them flexibly takes practice.

Pupils of different ages and abilities have their own mental images. It is the responsibility of the teacher to provide opportunities for pupils to discuss these images. Only through discussion does the teacher develop an insight into pupils' mental computational strategies while the pupils themselves need this opportunity to articulate their abstract mental processes.

Using this book

This book is a resource for practice and consolidation, from which pupils are able to enhance their understanding of strategies for mental calculations. It is assumed that teachers will have taught the basis strategies and concepts covered. The range of mental maths activities included here is appropriate for 9–10 year olds, though individual teachers or schools may decide to use it for other year groups (e.g. the more able pupils 8–9 year olds or the less able 10–11 year old pupils).

There are 30 exercises, to be used across the school year providing ten per term, with each set of ten focusing on a similar range of concepts. This allows for consolidation before moving on.

Each exercise is further divided into four sections, A-D, so each section can be treated as approximately ten minutes' daily practice. Sets A and C provide fifteen calculations covering place value and whole number, and the four operations, with particular reference to the signs and symbols associated with these calculations. At the end of each section is an extension activity for those pupils who finish quickly, often in the form of an investigation. Sets B and D include a range of word-associated problems, many in the context of shape, space and measures.

Mental calculation strategies

Pupils' mental strategies are based on an awareness of the number system, and number operations, their recall of number facts, and the ability to make sense of number problems. A range of strategies which pupils need to be taught in order to refine their methods of calculating are provided below:

Addition and subtraction
- When adding two sets, count on from the total in the first set, i.e 5 here..6, 7 (to add on 2)
- Start with the largest number first
- Count on or back in repeated steps
- Know that 7 + 2 is the same as 2 + 7
- Know that the difference between two numbers can be approached by looking at what needs to be added to the smaller number to make the larger one.
- Use two stages to add 9 (i.e. + 10 − 1) and subtract 9 (i.e.+ 10 + 1)
- Use two stages to add 11 (i.e. + 10 + 1) and subtract 11 (i.e. −10 − 1)
- Know that pairs of digits can be manipulated without affecting the total, e.g. 69 + 21 is the same as 70 + 20, thus helping to create more 'friendly' pairs
- Know doubles, e.g. 3 + 3
- Know near doubles, based on doubles already known, e.g. 3 + 4 is one more than 3 + 3
- Know facts that are two apart and can be transformed into doubles, e.g. 9 + 11 = 10 + 10

Patterns
e.g. 8 + 0 = 8   5 + 2 = 7
      7 + 1 = 8   2 + 5 = 7
      6 + 2 = 8   7 − 5 = 2
      5 + 3 = 8   7 − 2 = 5

Multiples of 10
- Adding any multiple of 10 to a single digit number does not change the unit number, e.g. 6 + 2 = 8
      6 + 12 = 18

- Adding any multiple of 10 to a number does not change the unit number,
  e.g. 16 + 20 = 36
        16 + 30 = 46

Partitioning into 5 and 10 when adding
- Partition 6, 7, 8 or 9 into '5 and something', e.g.

```
     8      +      6
(5 + 3)    +   (5 + 1)
(5 + 5)    +   (3 + 1)
    10      +     4
          14
```

- Partition into '10 and something', e.g.

```
    16       +     13
(10 + 10)   +   (6 + 3)
    20       +     9
          29
```

Multiplication and division
- Know that 3 + 3 + 3 + 3 is the same as 4 x 3 (or 3 x 4)
- Know that every division fact has a corresponding multiplication fact, involving the same three numbers
- Use two stages to multiply by 5, i.e. x10, ÷2; and two stages to divide by 5, i.e. ÷10, x 2.

Progression and continuity

This book and the others in this series, contain mental maths exercises that have been carefully planned and graded. There are opportunities to revisit aspects of mental recall as well as cover new concepts. This spiral approach reinforces and develops mental strategies, both between exercises, and from one book to the next, placing an emphasis on continued accuracy, and progression.

Language of mathematics

Mental Maths Practice provides an opportunity for teachers to develop mental maths by presenting pupils with aural exercises, or by marking an exercise with the class and asking individual pupils to articulate their mental methods of computation. It is important for pupils to become good communicators of mathematics, able to clarify observations and discoveries, and convey their findings to others. Teachers must use a range of appropriate expressions; whilst accepting pupils' early mathematical vocabulary, they should also assist them in developing more formal mathematical language as it is required. For this reason, these exercises are phrased in various terms and styles.

Exercise 1

A

1. £3·25 + £0·43 = £3·68
2. 34 + 23 = 57
3. 36 ÷ 6 = 6
4. 27 + 6 = 33
5. 46 − 23 = 23
6. 4 × 5 = 20
7. 58 − 9 = 49
8. 349, 350, 351, 352
9. $\frac{1}{2} = \frac{4}{8}$
10. 48 + 13 = 61
11. 7 × 4 = 28
12. $\frac{1}{4}$ = 25 %
13. 12 + 12 = 24
14. −10 −9 −8 −7
15. 378, 382, 386, 390

Copy and complete.

+	4	6	7	9
3	7	9	10	12
8	12	14	15	17
5	9	11	12	14
11	15	17	18	20

B

1. Write three thousand eight hundred and fifty in numerals. 3850
2. Round 2438 to the nearest hundred. 2400
3. What is the value of 4 in 4263? four thousands or 4000
4. Is the answer to 327 + 219 nearer 500 or 600? 500
5. 1, 2 and 4 are all factors of 4.
6. There are 12 counters in a bag. 50% are green. How many are green? 6
7. Is 9 a prime number? no
8. Continue the pattern: 16, 8, 4, 2, 1
9. Linda had 42 chickens. 17 eggs hatched. How many chickens does she have now? 59
10. There are 7 petals on a flower. If there are 63 petals, how many flowers will there be? 9
11. What is the change from £2·00 after spending £1·40? 60p
12. Noel drank 750 ml of a 2-litre bottle of orangeade. How much is left? 1250
13. Suzanne buys 4 packets of crisps at 25p each. How much does she spend? £1·00
14. Is an obtuse angle larger or smaller than 90°? larger
15. What is 21:45 written in 12-hour time? 9·45 pm

C

1. 9 × 2 = 18
2. £3·17 − £0·14 = £3·03
3. 40 ÷ 4 = 10
4. 72 + 26 = 98
5. 651, 650, 649, 648
6. £1·10 × 4 = £4·40
7. 14 ÷ 3 = 4 r 2
8. 72 − 9 − 7 = 56
9. 216 + 21 = 237
10. (15 ÷ 3) + 2 = 7
11. $\frac{1}{2}$ of 28 = 14
12. 734, 729, 724, 719
13. 53p + 44p = 97p
14. 6 + 7 + 4 + 5 = 22
15. 5 × 3 = 15

How many ways can you make $2\frac{1}{4}$? Here is one example.

$\frac{3}{4} + \frac{1}{2} + 1 = 2\frac{1}{4}$

D

1. Write 2420 in words.
   two thousand four hundred and twenty
2. 1005 plus sixteen = 1021
3. 2 thousands + 6 units + 4 tens = 2046
4. Is the answer to 58 − 19 nearer 50 or 40?
   40
5. Write the next multiple of 4:
   4, 8, 12, 16
6. Jerry ate 0·25 of a cake.
   Write what he ate as a fraction. $\frac{1}{4}$
7. 3^2 = 9
8. Put the following numbers in order, largest first: 1220, 1212, 1222, 1122
   1222, 1220, 1212, 1122
9. A mini-bus holds 8 passengers. How many mini-buses are needed to transport 32 children? 4
10. We blow up 58 balloons for a party. If 16 burst, how many are left? 42
11. What is the remainder when you divide 19 by 3? 1
12. 2 m 20 cm = 220 cm
13. I bought 2 kg of apples at 25p per kilo, and 1 kg of pears at 35p per kilo. How much did I spend? 85p
14. Hannah owes her mum £5·00. She gets £7·00 for her birthday, and pays her mum back. How much money does she have left? £2·00
15. Name this shape.
    (irregular) pentagon

Exercise 2

A

1. £4·26 + £0·52 = £4·78
2. 27 + 42 = 69
3. 56 ÷ 7 = 8
4. 43 + 9 = 52
5. 39 − 16 = 23
6. 6 × 7 = 42
7. 63 − 5 = 58
8. 473, 474, 475, 476
9. $\frac{1}{2} = \frac{2}{4}$
10. 39 + 22 = 61
11. 6 × 3 = 18
12. $\frac{1}{2}$ = 50 %
13. 16 + 42 = 58
14. −16 −15 −14 −13
15. 462, 465, 468, 471

⭐ Copy and complete the Decimal Function Machine **subtract 0·25**

in	out
5	4·75
4·5	4·25
1·75	1·5
3·25	3
2	1·75
4·25	4
6·5	6·25
3·35	3·1
2·75	2·5

B

1. Write four thousand six hundred and fifty-six in numerals.   4656
2. Round 2478 to the nearest 100.   2500
3. What is the value of 8 in 2486?   eight tens or 80
4. Is the answer to 193 + 524 nearer 600 or 700?   700
5. 1, 2 and 3 are all factors of 6.
6. There are 12 eggs in a box. 50% are brown. How many is this?   6
7. Is 6 a prime number?   no
8. Continue the pattern: 3, 6, 12, 24, 48
9. Frances collected 17 stamps. Her friend gave her 42 more. How many stamps does she have now?   59
10. There are 8 pages to a book. How many books can be made from 64 pages?   8
11. I have spent £1·85. What is my change from £2·00?   15p
12. Stephanie has cut 2·75 cm from a 4-metre length of ribbon. How much is left?   1·25 m
13. Brendan buys 6 bags of nuts at 20p each. How much does he spend?   £1·20
14. How many degrees in a right angle?   90°
15. What is 6:30 written in 24-hour time?   18·30

C

1. 5 × 3 = 15
2. £7·28 − £0·23 = £7·05
3. 24 ÷ 8 = 3
4. 54 + 25 = 79
5. 328, 327, 326, 325
6. £2·30 × 2 = £4·60
7. 21 ÷ 4 = 5 r 1
8. 54 − 3 − 5 = 46
9. 143 + 25 = 168
10. (15 ÷ 3) + 5 = 10
11. $\frac{1}{3}$ of 27 = 9
12. 529, 523, 517, 511
13. 26p + 35p = 61p
14. 3 + 9 + 5 + 7 = 24
15. 19 − 11 = 8

Copy and fill in the missing numbers.

```
   2 7 9
 + 4 6 5
   -----
   7 4 4
```

D

1. Write 3679 in words.
   three thousand six hundred and seventy-nine
2. 1116 plus twelve = 1128
3. 4 thousands + 6 tens + 4 units = 4064
4. Is the answer to 47 + 28 nearer 80 or 90? 80
5. Write the next multiple of 3:
   3, 6, 9, 12
6. Mark ate 0·5 of his sandwich. Write what he ate as a fraction. $\frac{1}{2}$
7. 2^2 = 4
8. Put these numbers in order, largest first:
   1329, 1239, 1293, 1932
   1932, 1329, 1293, 1239
9. Bread rolls come in packs of 12. How many packs must I buy to get 72 rolls? 6
10. 97 parents come to our school concert. If 65 are mums, how many are dads? 32
11. What is the remainder when you divide 28 by 8? 4
12. 4 m + 20 cm = 420 cm
13. I bought 5 kg of potatoes at 25p per kg and 1 kg of carrots at 50p per kg. How much did I spend? £1·75
14. The temperature was 2°C. During the night it dropped by 5°C. What was the lowest temperature? −3°C
15. Name this shape.
    parallelogram

Exercise 3

A

1. £1·72 + £0·23 = £1·95
2. 58 + 31 = 89
3. 36 ÷ 4 = 9
4. 19 + 4 = 23
5. 44 − 32 = 12
6. 5 × 8 = 40
7. 74 − 6 = 68
8. 627, 628, 629, 630
9. $\frac{1}{2} = \frac{3}{6}$
10. 27 + 44 = 71
11. 6 × 7 = 42
12. Write $\frac{1}{4}$ as a decimal. 0·25
13. 17 + 62 = 79
14. −20, −19, −18, −17
15. 591, 596, 601, 606

Use squared paper to plot the co-ordinates, then connect them in order.
(2,5) (1,3) (2,1) (3,3) (4,1) (5,3) (4,5) (3,3) (2,5)

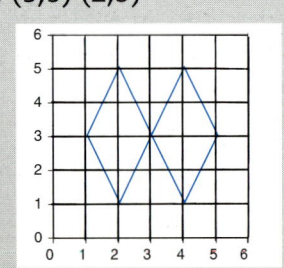

B

1. Write seven thousand and nine in numerals. 7009
2. Round 4268 to the nearest hundred. 4300
3. What is the value of 9 in 2972? nine hundreds or 900
4. Is the answer to 627 + 184 nearer 700 or 800? 800
5. 1, ☐ and 10 are all factors of 10. 2 or 5
6. There are 14 birds sitting on a wire. 50% fly away. How many are left? 7
7. Is 11 a prime number? yes
8. Continue the pattern: 1, 4, 7, 10, 13, 16
9. Sandra planted 25 bulbs and Liam planted 68 bulbs. How many bulbs did they plant altogether? 93
10. There are 6 mini-rolls in a pack. How many packs will hold 42 mini-rolls? 7
11. I spent £1·67. How much change did I get from £2·00? 33p
12. Ishmail has eaten 1 kg of apples from his 2 kg bag. How much is left? 1 kg
13. Dorina buys 6 packets of tissues at 25p each. How much does she spend? £1·50
14. How many degrees in a triangle? 180°
15. What is 22:00 written in 12-hour time? 10·00 pm

C

1. 4 × 7 = 28
2. £5·39 − £0·26 = £5·13
3. 27 ÷ 9 = 3
4. 34 + 42 = 76
5. 497, 496, 495, 494
6. £1·30 × 3 = £3·90
7. 26 ÷ 5 = 5 r 1
8. 68 − 6 − 4 = 58
9. 372 + 16 = 388
10. (20 ÷ 4) + 3 = 8
11. ¼ of 16 = 4
12. 627, 619, 611, 603
13. 42p + 27p = 69p
14. 6 + 6 + 5 + 9 = 26
15. 16 + 8 = 24

Can you make 48 using any of the four operations and some or all of these numbers?

3   4
   19
2
   25

D

1. Write 3840 in words.
   three thousand eight hundred and forty
2. 5554 plus thirty-four = 5588
3. 8 thousands + 7 hundreds + 2 tens + 9 units = 8729
4. Is the answer to 96 − 27 nearer 60 or 70? 70
5. Write the next multiple of 9: 45, 54, 63, 72
6. Frank bought 0·5 kg of bananas. Write this as a fraction. ½
7. 8^2 = 64
8. Put these numbers in order, smallest first: 2653, 2536, 3265, 3256
   2536, 2653, 3256, 3265
9. There are 32 children in our class, and 8 children in each group. How many groups are there? 4
10. 47 people are at the swimming pool. If 26 are in the shallow pool, how many are in the big pool? 21
11. What is the remainder when you divide 50 by 7? 1
12. 90 cm + 5 m = 590 cm
13. I bought 7 kg of carrots at 50p per kg, and 1 kg of pumpkin at 25p per kg. How much did I spend? £3·75
14. Su has £7·00. She wants to buy a bracelet that costs £10·00. How much more does she need? £3·00
15. Name this shape.   hexagon

Exercise 4

A

1. £5·24 + £0·35 = £5·59
2. 81 + 16 = 97
3. 45 ÷ 5 = 9
4. 38 + 5 = 43
5. 58 − 41 = 17
6. 9 × 3 = 27
7. 42 − 4 = 38
8. 194, 195, 196, 197
9. $\frac{1}{4} = \frac{2}{8}$
10. 58 + 33 = 91
11. 6 × 6 = 36
12. Write $\frac{1}{2}$ as a decimal. 0·5
13. 16 + 32 = 48
14. −18 −17 −16 −15
15. 236, 242, 248, 254

B

1. Write six thousand and twenty-seven in numerals. 6027
2. Round 3219 to the nearest 100. 3200
3. What is the value of 3 in 2239? three tens or 30
4. Is the answer to 175 + 238 nearer 300 or 400? 400
5. 1, 2, 3, 4, 6, 12 are all factors of 12.
6. There are 20 biscuits in a pack. 25% are chocolate. How many chocolate biscuits are there? 5
7. Is 3 a prime number? yes
8. Continue the pattern: 2, 7, 12, 17, 22
9. Veronica had 19 pairs of earrings. Her sister gave her 28 more pairs. How many pairs does she have now? 47
10. A window has 9 panes of glass in it. How many windows are there if there are 63 panes of glass? 7
11. I have spent £1·36. What is my change from £2·00? 64p
12. Oscar bought 8 ice-creams at 50p each. How much has he spent? £4·00
13. Ali poured out 1 litre from a 2-litre bottle of milk. How many ml are left? 1000 ml
14. How many degrees are there in a circle? 360°
15. What is 15:15 written in 12-hour time? 3·15 pm

Copy and complete.

−	6	10	11	9
12	6	2	1	3
18	12	8	7	9
17	11	7	6	8
14	8	4	3	5

C

1. 6 × 2 = 12
2. £4·28 − £0·15 = £4·13
3. 54 ÷ 9 = 6
4. 65 + 34 = 99
5. 368, 367, 366, 365
6. £1·20 × 4 = £4·80
7. 17 ÷ 2 = 8 r 1
8. 39 − 5 − 8 = 26
9. 843 + 35 = 878
10. (14 ÷ 7) + 2 = 4
11. $\frac{1}{5}$ of 30 = 6
12. 561, 557, 553, 549
13. 83p + 14p = 97p
14. 7 + 2 + 5 + 4 = 18
15. 6 × 4 = 24

How many ways can you make $5\frac{1}{2}$? Here is one example.

$3\frac{1}{4} + 2\frac{1}{4} = 5\frac{1}{2}$

D

1. Write 7342 in words.
   seven thousand three hundred and forty-two
2. 1872 plus fifteen = 1887
3. 6 hundreds + 4 thousands + 6 tens + 1 unit = 4661
4. Is the answer to 87 − 35 nearer 50 or 60? 50
5. Write the next multiple of 8: 56, 64, 72, 80
6. When Ingrid made a cake she mixed in 0·25 kg of butter. Write this as a fraction. $\frac{1}{4}$
7. 4^2 = 16
8. Put these numbers in order, largest first: 2917, 2197, 2791, 2971
   2971, 2917, 2791, 2197
9. If a car holds 5 people, how many cars are needed to transport 25 people? 5
10. Our bath holds about 42 litres. It is half full. How many more litres must I add to fill it? 21 litres
11. What is the remainder when you divide 17 by 4? 1
12. 8 m 40 cm = 840 cm
13. I bought 6 kg of apples at 30p per kilo and 1 kg of oranges at 20p per kilo. How much did I spend? £2·00
14. At 2 o'clock the temperature is − 5°C. By 10 o'clock it has dropped by a further 3°C. What is the new temperature? −8°C
15. Name this shape. (irregular) hexagon

Exercise 5

A

1. £2·43 + £0·26 = £2·69
2. 17 + 72 = 89
3. 16 ÷ 2 = 8
4. 47 + 8 = 55
5. 27 − 15 = 12
6. 3 × 8 = 24
7. 81 − 3 = 78
8. 871, 872, 873, 874
9. $\frac{2}{4} = \frac{1}{2}$
10. 69 + 32 = 101
11. 8 × 3 = 24
12. $\frac{1}{5}$ = 20 %
13. 32 + 11 = 43
14. −17 −16 −15 −14
15. 627, 631, 635, 639

Copy and complete
the Decimal Function Machine
Add 0·25

in	out
1·45	1·7
3·25	3·5
4·5	4·75
2	2·25
1·35	1·6
5·25	5·5
3·5	3·75
4	4·25
2·45	2·7

B

1. Write eight thousand four hundred and twenty-nine in numerals.   8429
2. Round 3692 to the nearest 100.   3700
3. What is the value of 8 in 8292?
   eight thousand or 8000
4. Is the answer to 387 + 496 nearer 800 or 900?   900
5. 1, 2, 4 and 8 are all factors of 8.
6. There are 8 candles in a box.
   25% of them are green.
   How many green candles are there?   2
7. Is 13 a prime number?   yes
8. Continue the pattern:
   6, 10, 14, 18, 22
9. Tim has 36 books and Farah has 39 books. How many do they have altogether?   75
10. There are 10 ice-lollies in a box. How many boxes will be needed for 40 lollies?   4
11. What is the change from £2·50 after spending £2·41?   9p
12. Dorothy has 5 m of material. She uses 2·25 m to make a skirt. How much is left?   2 m 75 cm or 2·75 m
13. Mohammed buys 7 chocolate bars at 25p each. How much does he spend?   £1·75
14. Are the angles of an equilateral triangle larger or smaller than 90°?   smaller
15. What is 17:10 in 12-hour time?   5·10 pm

C

1. 4 × 8 = 32
2. £6·43 − £0·31 = £6·12
3. 24 ÷ 2 = 12
4. 42 + 37 = 79
5. 502, 501, 500, 499
6. £2·40 × 2 = £4·80
7. 20 ÷ 3 = 6 r 2
8. 42 − 7 − 3 = 32
9. 673 + 16 = 689
10. (12 ÷ 6) + 5 = 7
11. $\frac{1}{7}$ of 28 = 4
12. 935, 929, 923, 917
13. 62p + 27p = 89p
14. 3 + 2 + 9 + 8 = 22
15. 12 × 2 = 24

Copy and fill in the missing numbers.

```
   7 9 3
 −  2 5 8
 ─────────
   5 3 5
```

D

1. Write 9278 in words.
   nine thousand two hundred and seventy eight
2. 5764 plus fifteen = 5779
3. 6 units + 3 thousands + 4 tens + 8 hundreds = 3846
4. Is the answer to 69 + 23 nearer 90 or 100? 90
5. Write the next multiple of 6: 36, 42, 48, 54
6. Topi gave 0·75 of her sweets to James. Write this as a fraction. $\frac{3}{4}$
7. 9^2 = 81
8. Put these numbers in order, largest first: 3748, 3874, 3487, 3784
   3874, 3784, 3748, 3487
9. At a banquet 6 people sat at each table. How many tables were needed to seat 54 people? 9
10. A bus holds 65 passengers. If 33 are downstairs, how many are upstairs? 32
11. What is the remainder when you divide 17 by 2? 1
12. 2 m + 90 cm = 290 cm
13. I bought 3 kg of pears at 40p per kilo, and 1 kg of plums at 60p per kilo. How much did I spend? £1·80
14. Margaret owes Mary £9·00. She gets £12·00 pocket money and pays Mary back. How much has she now? £3·00
15. Name this shape. regular hexagon

Exercise 6

A

1. £6·34 + £0·41 = £6·75
2. 68 + 12 = 80
3. 27 ÷ 3 = 9
4. 25 + 7 = 32
5. 74 − 32 = 42
6. 7 × 7 = 49
7. 28 − 9 = 19
8. 528, 529, 530, 531
9. $\frac{1}{3} = \frac{2}{6}$
10. 87 + 14 = 101
11. 2 × 10 = 20
12. Write $\frac{1}{5}$ as a decimal. 0·2
13. 47 + 44 = 91
14. −12 −11 −10 −9
15. 891, 895, 899, 903

Use squared paper to plot the co-ordinates, then connect them in order.

(0,5) (1,2) (2,5) (3,2) (4,5) (5,2) (6,5)

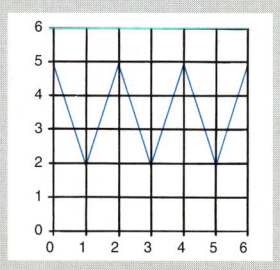

B

1. Write six thousand seven hundred and thirty-one in numerals. 6731
2. Round 6396 to the nearest 100. 6400
3. What is the value of 4 in 6714? four units or 4
4. Is the answer to 576 − 258 nearer 300 or 400? 300
5. 1, 2, 4, 8, 16 are all factors of 16.
6. There are four batteries in a pack. Only 25% of them work. How many batteries work? 1
7. Is 17 a prime number? yes
8. Continue the pattern: 21, 42, 63, 84, 105.
9. Anthony has been on the train for 23 minutes. He will be on the train for 19 minutes more. How long is his journey altogether? 42 minutes
10. There are 8 balloons to a bag. How many bags will hold 48 balloons? 6
11. What change will you get from £2·50 if you spend £2·37? 13p
12. Francesca bought a 2 kg jar of sweets. 750 g were toffees. How many grams were not toffees? 1250 g
13. Pedro saved 15p a day for four days. How much did he save? 60p
14. How many degrees are there between 12 and 3 on a clock (going clockwise)? 90°
15. What is 20:25 written in 12-hour time? 8·25 pm

C

1. 6 × 6 = 36
2. £8·28 − £0·11 = £8·17
3. 90 ÷ 10 = 9
4. 61 + 28 = 89
5. 703, 702, 701, 700
6. £3·10 × 5 = £15·50
7. 22 ÷ 3 = 7 r 1
8. 52 − 6 − 8 = 38
9. 435 + 44 = 479
10. (18 ÷ 3) + 2 = 8
11. $\frac{1}{10}$ of 30 = 3
12. 621, 618, 615, 612
13. 43p + 31p = 74p
14. 6 + 8 + 4 + 2 = 20
15. 19 − 10 = 9

Can you make 78 using any of the four operations and some or all of these numbers?

3, 5, 33, 6, 16

D

1. Write 8514 in words.
   eight thousand five hundred and fourteen
2. 3762 plus thirty-four = 3796
3. 7 hundreds + 2 units + 3 tens + 1 thousand = 1732
4. Is the answer to 53 + 36 nearer 80 or 90? 90
5. Write the next multiple of 4: 16, 20, 24, 28
6. Elizabeth is given 0·25 of a cake. Write this as a fraction. $\frac{1}{4}$
7. 6^2 = 36
8. Put these numbers in order, largest first: 3826, 3286, 3682, 3268
   3826, 3682, 3286, 3268
9. In a hotel there were 9 rooms on each floor. If there were 45 rooms, how many floors were there? 5
10. A maths lesson lasts 45 minutes. If we have been working for 32 minutes, how long will it be before we finish? 13 minutes
11. What is the remainder when you divide 56 by 9? 2
12. 7 m + 45 cm = 745 cm
13. I bought 2 kg of beans at 25p per kilo, and 2 kg of broccoli at 25p per kilo. How much did I spend? £1·00
14. At 7 o'clock the temperature was −4°C. By 12 o'clock it was 4°C. By how many degrees has the temperature risen? 8°C
15. Draw a pentagon. any five-sided shape

Exercise 7

A

1. £8·72 + £0·23 = £8·95
2. 43 + 35 = 78
3. 55 ÷ 5 = 11
4. 36 + 5 = 41
5. 68 − 45 = 23
6. 2 × 7 = 14
7. 33 − 6 = 27
8. 738, 739, 740, 741
9. $\frac{1}{5} = \frac{3}{15}$
10. 78 + 13 = 91
11. 3 × 9 = 27
12. $\frac{3}{4}$ = 75 %
13. 23 + 44 = 67
14. −14, −13, −12, −11
15. 746, 751, 756, 761

Copy and complete.

×	16	8	7	6
4	64	32	28	24
9	144	72	63	54
3	48	24	21	18
10	160	80	70	60

B

1. Write four thousand and forty in numerals.
   4040
2. Round 2621 to the nearest 100.   2600
3. What is the value of 7 in 7992?
   seven thousand or 7000
4. Is the answer to 892 − 119 nearer 800 or 700?   800
5. 1, 2, 7, 14 are all factors of 14.
6. 30 children go on a picnic. 50% have cherryade to drink. How many drink cherryade?   15
7. Is 21 a prime number?   no
8. Continue the pattern: 20, 40, 80, 160, 320
9. There are 38 people on a bus. At the bus stop 19 people get on. How many passengers are there now?   57
10. There are 7 days in a week. How many weeks in 56 days?   8
11. What change do I get from £2·50 when I have spent £2·27?   23p
12. A 5-litre container has $3\frac{3}{4}$ litres of water in it. How much more water is needed to fill it?
    $1\frac{1}{4}$ litres or 1250 ml
13. Jerome spends 25p each day for 5 days. How much does he spend altogether?   £1·25
14. How many degrees are there between 3 and 9 on a clock face?   180°
15. What is 14:15 written in 12-hour time?
    2·15 pm

C

1. 6 × 8 = 48
2. £7·49 − £0·27 = £7·22
3. 18 ÷ 2 = 9
4. 36 + 11 = 47
5. 240, 239, 238, 237
6. £2·10 × 6 = £12·60
7. 15 ÷ 2 = 7 r 1
8. 93 − 8 − 7 = 78
9. 856 + 41 = 897
10. (24 ÷ 2) + 4 = 16
11. $\frac{1}{6}$ of 42 = 7
12. 418, 413, 408, 403
13. 72p + 16p = 88p
14. 8 + 5 + 7 + 6 = 26
15. 16 + 8 = 24

How many ways can you make $4\frac{3}{4}$? Here is one example.

$7 - 2\frac{1}{4} = 4\frac{3}{4}$

D

1. Write 6354 in words. six thousand three hundred and fifty-four
2. 4781 plus sixteen = 4797
3. 5 thousands + 4 hundreds + 6 units + 9 tens = 5496
4. Is the answer to 67 − 48 nearer 30 or 20? 20
5. Write the next multiple of 7: 21, 28, 35, 42
6. Aaron spent 0·75 of his pocket money. Write what he spent as a fraction. $\frac{3}{4}$
7. 10^2 = 100
8. Put these numbers in order, largest first: 5616, 5661, 6561, 6165
   6561, 6165, 5661, 5616
9. There were 7 questions on each page of a test paper. If there were 35 questions altogether, how many pages were there? 5
10. 60 cakes are baked for a party. When 52 have been eaten, how many are left? 8
11. What is the remainder when you divide 32 by 3? 2
12. 9 m + 75 cm = 975 cm
13. I bought 5 kg of oranges at 50p per kilo, and 1 kg of mandarins at 50p per kilo. How much did I spend? £3·00
14. Simon owes his brother £15·00. He earns £30·00 and pays his brother back. How much has Simon left? £15·00
15. Name this shape. (regular) hexagon

Exercise 8

A

1. £9·28 + £0·61 = £9·89
2. 86 + 13 = 99
3. 32 ÷ 4 = 8
4. 52 + 9 = 61
5. 94 − 71 = 23
6. 8 × 9 = 72
7. 93 − 7 = 86
8. 239, 240, 241, 242
9. $\frac{1}{3} = \frac{2}{6}$
10. 38 + 24 = 62
11. 5 × 5 = 25
12. Write $\frac{3}{4}$ as a decimal. 0·75
13. 35 + 63 = 98
14. −19 −18 −17 −16
15. 925, 930, 935, 940

Copy and complete the Decimal Function Machine subtract 0·75

in	out
1·45	0·7
2	1·25
4·75	4
1·25	0·5
2·9	2·15
3·9	3·15
5	4·25
3·5	2·75
4·25	3·5

B

1. Write five thousand and sixty-eight in numerals. 5068
2. Round 8629 to the nearest 1000. 9000
3. What is the value of 1 in 8619? ten units or 10
4. Is the answer to 712 − 189 nearer 500 or 600? 500
5. 1, 2, 4, 5, 10 and 20 are all factors of 20.
6. Out of 36 oranges, 50% have seeds in them. How many oranges have seeds? 18
7. Is 15 a prime number? No
8. Continue the pattern: 3, 6, 12, 24, 48, 96
9. Leroy walked 26 km on Thursday and another 49 km on Friday. How many km did he walk altogether? 75 km
10. There are 81 flowers to be put into bunches of 9 flowers each. How many bunches will this be? 9
11. What is left from £2·50 after I have spent £1·85? 65p
12. Zena saved 20p a week for 8 weeks. How much did she save? £1·60
13. Gita had 225 cm left from a 10-metre piece of ribbon. How much did she use? 775 cm or 7·75 m
14. How many degrees are there between 12 and 9 on a clock, going clockwise? 270
15. What is 23:55 written in 12-hour time? 11·55 pm

C

1. 7 × 7 = 49
2. £9·87 − £0·65 = £9·22
3. 18 ÷ 3 = 6
4. 53 + 26 = 79
5. 802, 801, 800, 799
6. £2·20 × 3 = £6·60
7. 32 ÷ 5 = 6 r 2
8. 47 − 6 − 9 = 32
9. 156 + 23 = 179
10. (28 ÷ 7) + 3 = 7
11. $\frac{1}{4}$ of 32 = 8
12. 445, 437, 429, 421
13. 35p + 44p = 79p
14. 3 + 5 + 9 + 7 = 24
15. 14 + 7 = 21

Copy and fill in the missing numbers.

```
    9 3 4
  ×     9
  -------
  8 4 0 6
```

D

1. Write 4989 in words.
   four thousand nine hundred and eighty nine
2. 1648 plus thirteen = 1661
3. 5 thousands + 6 hundreds + 3 units = 5603
4. Is the answer to 43 − 12 nearer 30 or 20? 30
5. Write the next multiple of 2: 8, 10, 12, 14
6. Rowena was given 0·5 of an apple. Write this as a fraction. $\frac{1}{2}$
7. 1^2 = 1
8. Put these numbers in order, smallest first: 6719, 6791, 6971, 6917
   6719, 6791, 6917, 6971
9. Each shelf in a bookcase holds 6 books. If there are 60 books, how many shelves are there? 10
10. Mum washed 25 shirts. She has ironed 17. How many are left to iron? 8
11. What is the remainder when you divide 79 by 2? 1
12. 84 cm + 3 m = 384 cm
13. I bought 4 kg of potatoes at 25p per kilo, and 1 kg of parsnips at 50p per kilo. How much did I spend? £1·50
14. The temperature was −6°C. Then it rose by 4°C. What is the new temperature? −2°C
15. Name this shape. (regular) pentagon

Exercise 9

A

1. £7·41 + £0·28 = £7·69
2. 75 + 11 = 86
3. 48 ÷ 6 = 8
4. 62 + 8 = 70
5. 88 − 43 = 45
6. 6 × 3 = 18
7. 61 − 5 = 56
8. 634, 635, 636, 637
9. $\frac{1}{4} = \frac{2}{8}$
10. 59 + 11 = 70
11. 4 × 9 = 36
12. Write $\frac{1}{3}$ as a decimal. 0·33
13. 42 + 23 = 65
14. −15, −14, −13, −12
15. 463, 469, 475, 481

Use squared paper to plot the co-ordinates, then connect them in order.
(1,−1) (2,−3) (1,−5) (4,−5) (3,−3) (4,−1) (1,−1)

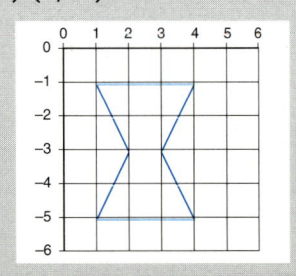

B

1. Write two thousand nine hundred and forty-seven in numerals. 2947
2. Round 5852 to the nearest 100. 5900
3. What is the value of 1 in 2160? one hundred or 100
4. Is the answer to 985 − 219 nearer 800 or 700? 800
5. 1, 2, 3, 6, 9, 18 are all factors of 18.
6. Of 40 people in a cinema queue, 25% are wearing hats. How many people are wearing hats? 10
7. Is 19 a prime number? yes
8. Continue the pattern: 48, 24, 12, 6, 3
9. 66 people visited an exhibition on the opening day and 38 people the day after. How many visitors were there altogether? 104
10. Each train carriage can seat 8 people. How many carriages will seat 56 people? 7
11. What is left from £2·50 after you have spent £1·69? 81p
12. Marianne spends 50p on a magazine every week for 10 weeks. How much does she spend altogether? £5·00
13. If Jeremy spills of a 1-litre bottle of cola, how many ml did he spill? 1000 ml
14. How many degrees are there between 2 and 8 on a clock? 180°
15. What is 13:40 written in 12-hour time? 1·40 pm

C

1. 6 × 4 = 24
2. £4·65 − £0·43 = £4·22
3. 72 ÷ 8 = 9
4. 85 + 14 = 99
5. 499, 498, 497, 496
6. £4·10 × 3 = £12·30
7. 11 ÷ 2 = 5 r 1
8. 87 − 9 − 3 = 75
9. 732 + 67 = 799
10. (24 ÷ 6) + 7 = 11
11. $\frac{1}{8}$ of 40 = 5
12. 629, 623, 617, 611
13. 14p + 55p = 69p
14. 8 + 1 + 9 + 2 = 20
15. 5 × 4 = 20

Can you make 25 using any of the four operations and some or all of these numbers?

4   7
    9
16
    48

D

1. Write 5421 in words.
   five thousand four hundred and twenty-one
2. 4651 plus eighteen = 4669
3. 9 thousands + 5 hundreds + 7 tens = 9570
4. Is the answer to 76 − 25 nearer 50 or 60? 50
5. Write the next multiple of 5: 5, 10, 15, 20
6. Jane ate 0·75 of her lunch. What fraction did she eat? $\frac{3}{4}$
7. 7^2 = 49
8. Put these numbers in order, largest first:
   1658, 1865, 1586, 1856
   1865, 1856, 1658, 1586
9. Bananas come in bunches of 4. How many bunches are needed to feed one to each of 32 monkeys? 8
10. Joey has to deliver 56 newspapers. How many has he left when he has delivered 25? 31
11. What is the remainder when you divide 47 by 6? 5
12. 6 m + 70 cm = 670 cm
13. I bought 4 kg of plums at 80p per kilo, and 1 kg of peaches at 60p per kilo. How much did I spend? £3·80
14. David owes his Dad £6·00. His mum gives him £10·00. How much has he left, after he has paid back the money to his Dad? £4·00
15. Name this shape. (irregular) hexagon

Exercise 10

A

1. £5·53 + £0·26 = £5·79
2. 94 + 15 = 109
3. 63 ÷ 7 = 9
4. 78 + 6 = 84
5. 57 − 21 = 36
6. 9 × 4 = 36
7. 45 − 6 = 39
8. 942, 943, 944, 945
9. $\frac{1}{5} = \frac{2}{10}$
10. 29 + 41 = 70
11. 11 × 3 = 33
12. $\frac{1}{3}$ = 33 %
13. 68 + 23 = 91
14. −11, −10, −9, −8
15. 184, 187, 190, 193

B

1. Write one thousand one hundred and six in numerals. 1106
2. Round 1275 to the nearest 100. 1300
3. What is the value of 6 in 1695? six hundred or 600
4. Is the answer to 189 + 227 nearer 400 or 500? 400
5. 1, 3, and 9 are all factors of 9.
6. Of 20 children in a class, 50% are boys. How many is this? 10
7. Is 7 a prime number? Yes
8. Continue the pattern: 1, 2, 4, 8, 16, 32
9. Sanjay picked 35 apples and Veejay picked 26 more. How many apples did they pick altogether? 61
10. If each cake tin holds 9 cakes, how many tins are needed for 54 cakes? 6
11. What change do I get from £2·00 if I spend £1·55? 45p
12. Shane has used 2 kg of a 3 kg bag of flour, how many grams are left? 1000 g
13. Sherelle buys 6 packets of sweets at 50p each. How much does she spend altogether? £3·00
14. Is an acute angle larger or smaller than 90 degrees? smaller
15. What is 18:30 written in 12-hour time? 6·30 pm

Copy and complete.

÷	4	8	2	1
16	4	2	8	16
40	10	5	20	40
24	6	3	12	24
32	8	4	16	32

C

1. 5 × 5 = 25
2. £5·47 − £0·25 = £5·22
3. 33 ÷ 3 = 11
4. 47 + 21 = 68
5. 352, 351, 350, 349
6. £3·20 × 2 = £6·40
7. 19 ÷ 4 = 4 r 3
8. 64 − 8 − 4 = 52
9. 546 + 45 = 591
10. (30 ÷ 10) + 4 = 7
11. $\frac{1}{9}$ of 63 = 7
12. 417, 411, 405, 399
13. 81p + 16p = 97p
14. 7 + 6 + 9 + 8 = 30
15. 17 − 8 = 9

How many ways can you make $5\frac{1}{2}$? Here is one example.

$2\frac{1}{2} + 1\frac{3}{4} + 1\frac{1}{4} = 5\frac{1}{2}$

D

1. Write 1605 in words.
   one thousand six hundred and five
2. 3758 plus eleven = 3769
3. 3 thousands + 4 hundreds + 3 tens + 2 units = 3432
4. Is the answer to 73 + 16 nearer 80 or 90? 90
5. Write the next multiple of 6: 6, 12, 18, 24
6. Jamal lost 0·25 of his pocket money. Write what he lost as a fraction. $\frac{1}{4}$
7. 5^2 = 25
8. Put these numbers in order, largest first: 1612, 1126, 1216, 1621
   1621, 1612, 1216, 1126
9. Squash comes in 2-litre bottles. How many bottles will hold 18 litres of squash? 9
10. A shop has 36 loaves of bread. When 14 are sold, how many are left? 22
11. What is the remainder when you divide 23 by 5? 3
12. 3 m + 30 cm = 330 cm
13. I bought 3 kg of oranges at 40p per kilo, and 2 kg of bananas at 60p per kilo. How much did I spend? £2·40
14. The temperature was −3°C before it dropped another 2°C. What is the temperature now? −5°C
15. Draw an octagon. any eight-sided closed shape

Exercise 11

A

1. £4·60 + £1·29 = £5·89
2. 65 + 16 = 81
3. 56 ÷ [7] = 8
4. [9] + 16 = 25
5. 45 − [7] = 38
6. [6] × 2 = 12
7. 67 − 19 = 48
8. 385, 384, 383, [382]
9. 0·25 = $\frac{[1]}{4}$
10. [3] × [6] = 18 or others
11. 27 + 9 + 3 = 39
12. (4 × 3) − 9 = 3
13. $\frac{1}{2}$ of 16 = 8
14. −12 −9 −6 [−3]
15. 479, 475, 471, [467]

Copy and complete
the Decimal Function Machine
add 1·5

in	out
2·75	4·25
4·6	6·1
3·5	5
1·25	2·75
3	4·5
4·75	6·25
5·5	7
2	3·5
5·8	7·3

B

1. Put these numbers in order, smallest first:
   127, 3171, 107, 3072
   107, 127, 3072, 3171
2. Continue the pattern: 7, 11, 15, 19, [23], [27]
3. Round 11 627 to the nearest 1000   12 000
4. Thirty-six plus fifty-four = ninety
5. How many even numbers are there between 27 and 53?   13
6. 2[3] + 9 = 32
7. 5^2 + 7 = 32
8. In a traffic survey, some children counted 39 cars on Monday and 84 cars on Tuesday. How many cars did they count altogether?   123
9. Sasha picked 72 apples and put them into bags.
   If each bag holds 9 apples, how many bags did she fill?   8
10. 3, 1, 9 are all factors of which number?   9
11. $\frac{3}{4} = \frac{[6]}{8}$
12. What is my change from £5·00 after I have spent £4·57?   43p
13. How many oranges at 32p each can I buy with £1·00?   3
14. Draw an isosceles triangle.
15. A clock shows 3·10. It is 20 minutes slow. What is the correct time?   3·30

C

1. 6 × ⬚2⬚ = 12
2. £4·69 − £1·27 = £3·42
3. ⬚36⬚ ÷ 6 = 6
4. 28 + ⬚31⬚ = 59
5. 3761, 3762, ⬚3763⬚, 3764
6. £4·13 × 2 = £8·26
7. 17 ÷ 4 = 4 r 1
8. 53 − 4 − ⬚7⬚ = 42
9. 315 + 243 = 558
10. (18 ÷ 6) − 2 = 1
11. 25% of ⬚100⬚ = 25
12. 256, ⬚261⬚, 266, 271
13. 36p + 27p = 63p
14. 9 + 3 + 4 + 12 = 28
15. 27 ⬚+⬚ 9 = 36

Copy and fill in the missing numbers.

25⬚5⬚3 ÷ 37 = 69

D

1. Write forty-two thousand, three hundred and seventy-nine as a number. 42379
2. 4 × 2 × 3 = 24
3. Imagine a 0 to 99 number square. Which number is directly below 36? 46
4. Which number is not a multiple of 4? 48, 46, 40, 44, 52? 46
5. Two numbers multiplied together make 56. If one of them is 8, what is the other? 7
6. What is the sum of thirty-eight and seventy-five? one hundred and thirteen
7. Estimate 479 + 342 to the nearest ten. 820
8. $\frac{1}{5}$ of 100 = 20
9. There were 72 plants in a greenhouse. 45 of them died. How many were left? 27
10. Put these fractions in order, smallest first: $\frac{1}{4}$
    $\frac{1}{3}$ $\frac{1}{16}$ $\frac{1}{16}$ $\frac{1}{4}$ $\frac{1}{3}$
11. 3 m − 20 cm = ⬚280⬚ cm
12. Share 25p and 15p equally between 2 children. How much does each child get? 20p
13. Candles come in boxes of 8. How many candles are there are in 9 boxes? 72
14. If 1st January is a Monday, what day is 4th January? Thursday
15. What is the perimeter of this shape? 16 cm   4 cm / 4 cm

Exercise 12

A

1. £3·40 + £1·27 = £4·67
2. 47 + 25 = 72
3. 27 ÷ [3] = 9
4. 18 + [8] = 26
5. [39] − 18 = 21
6. 5 × [7] = 35
7. 72 − 53 = 19
8. [563], 562, 561, 560
9. 0·5 = $\frac{[1]}{[2]}$
10. [6] × [9] = 54 (or 9 × 6)
11. 35 + 6 + 4 = 45
12. (6 × 5) − 4 = 26
13. $\frac{1}{4}$ of 12 = 3
14. −16 −14 [−12] −10
15. 362, [359], 356, 353

Use squared paper to plot the co-ordinates, then connect them in order.

(1,−1) (1,−6) (2,−4) (3,−6)
(4,−4) (5,−6) (5,−1) (4,−3)
(3,−1) (2,−3) (1,−1)

B

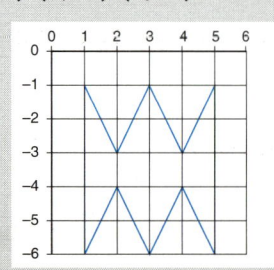

1. Put these numbers in order, smallest first:
   2794, 362, 4284, 987   362, 987, 2794, 4284
2. Continue the pattern: 66, 55, 44, [33], [22]
3. Round 14 262 to the nearest 1000   14 000
4. Eighty-six plus twelve = ninety-eight
5. How many odd numbers are there between 36 and 62?   13
6. 3[2] + 7 = 39
7. 6^2 − 5 = 31
8. Last week the shopkeeper sold 46 bottles of ketchup. This week he sold 29 bottles. How many has he sold altogether?   75
9. A farmer collected 54 eggs from her hens. How many boxes of 6 did these fill?   9
10. 2, 12, 6, 3, 1, 4 are factors of which number?   12
11. $\frac{1}{3} = \frac{[2]}{6}$
12. What is my change from £5·00 after I have spent £4·23?   77p
13. How many pencils at 17p each can I buy with £1·00?   5
14. Draw a regular octagon.
15. A clock shows 25 past 11. It is 15 minutes fast. What is the correct time?   10 past 11 or 11·10

C

1. 2 × ☐7☐ = 14

2. £3·45 − £2·24 = £1·21

3. ☐35☐ ÷ 5 = 7

4. 43 + ☐33☐ = 76

5. 9878, 9879, ☐9880☐, 9881

6. £3·12 × 3 = £9·36

7. 19 ÷ 3 = 6 r 1

8. 29 − 6 − ☐7☐ = 16

9. 823 + 152 = 975

10. (24 ÷ 3) − 5 = 3

11. 50% of ☐200☐ = 100

12. 379, 385, ☐391☐, 397

13. 43p + 28p = 71p

14. 7 + 3 + 4 + 16 = 30

15. 16 ☐÷☐ 4 = 4

Can you make 408 using any of the four operations and some or all of these numbers? 8, 4, 41, 5, 39

D

1. Write twenty-seven thousand, two hundred and six as a number. 27 206

2. 4 × 5 × 3 = 60

3. Imagine a 0 to 99 number square. Which number is directly above 72? 62

4. Which number is not a multiple of 7? 63, 49, 74, 77, 70? 74

5. Two numbers multiplied together make 72. If one of them is 9, what is the other? 8

6. What is the sum of sixty-four and twenty-nine? ninety-three

7. Estimate 376 + 498 to the nearest ten. 870

8. $\frac{1}{10}$ of 100 = 10

9. A shop had 85 cushions in stock. 28 were sold. How many were left? 57

10. Put these fractions in order, smallest first: $\frac{1}{6}$ $\frac{1}{9}$ $\frac{1}{7}$ $\frac{1}{9}$ $\frac{1}{7}$ $\frac{1}{6}$

11. 2 litres − 700 ml = ☐1300☐ ml

12. Share 16p and 12p equally between 2 children. How much does each child get? 14p

13. There are 6 mini-buses going to the zoo, with 9 children in each. How many children are going to the zoo? 54

14. If 9th April is a Saturday, what day is 13th April? Wednesday

15. What is the perimeter of this shape? 24 cm (4 cm by 8 cm rectangle)

Exercise 13

A

1. £ 2·90 + £1·08 = £3·98
2. 73 + 18 = 91
3. 36 ÷ [6] = 6
4. 27 + [5] = 32
5. [34] – 9 = 25
6. 4 × [9] = 36
7. 95 – 27 = 68
8. 971, [970], 969, 968
9. 0·33 = [33] %
10. [4] × [6] = 24 or other
11. 52 + 7 + 2 = 61
12. (8 × 4) – 3 = 29
13. $\frac{1}{5}$ of 60 = 12
14. –21 [–18] –15 –12
15. 541, 536, 531, [526]

Copy and complete.

+	17	13	14	16
12	29	25	26	28
10	27	23	24	26
15	32	28	29	31
11	28	24	25	27

B

1. Put these numbers in order, smallest first: 2621, 621, 6212, 216   216, 621, 2621, 6212
2. Continue the pattern: 66, 72, 78, [84], [90]
3. Round 11 512 to the nearest 1000.   12 000
4. Twenty-three plus forty-nine = seventy-two
5. How many even numbers are there between 17 and 39?   11
6. 5[7] + 6 = 63
7. 4^2 + 9 = 25
8. Last night Mehmet read 52 pages of his book. This morning he read 19 more. How many pages has he read?   71
9. At a party, how many biscuits will each child get if there are 36 biscuits and 6 children?   6
10. 5, 1, 3, 15 are factors of which number?   15
11. $\frac{2}{10}$ = $\frac{[1]}{5}$
12. What is my change from £5·00 after I have spent £4·11?   89p
13. How many chocolate bars at 27p each can I buy with £1·00?   3
14. Draw a right-angled triangle.
15. The time on a clock is 5 to 6. If the clock is 5 minutes slow, what is the correct time?   6·00

C

1. 7 × [3] = 21

2. £6·29 − £4·16 = £2·13

3. [27] ÷ 3 = 9

4. 74 + [21] = 95

5. 5427, 5428, 5429, [5430]

6. £2·21 × 4 = £8·84

7. 42 ÷ 5 = 8 r [2]

8. 37 − 8 − [7] = 22

9. 372 + 314 = 686

10. (40 ÷ 5) − 2 = 6

11. 25% of [400] = 100

12. 466, 475, 484, [493]

13. 29p + 23p = 52p

14. 8 + 5 + 4 + 12 = 29

15. 54 [−] 7 = 47

How many ways can you make $6\frac{1}{3}$? Here is one example.

$$10 - 3\frac{2}{3} = 6\frac{1}{3}$$

D

1. Write sixteen thousand and seven as a number. 16 007

2. 6 × 2 × 5 = 60

3. Imagine a 0 to 99 number square. Which number is one square to the right of 8? 9

4. Which number is not a multiple of 6? 62, 66, 72, 60, 78? 62

5. Two numbers multiplied together make 27. If one of them is 3, what is the other? 9

6. What is the sum of forty-six and fifty-nine? one hundred and five

7. Estimate 308 + 487 to the nearest ten. 790 or 800

8. $\frac{1}{3}$ of 90 = 30

9. There are 84 paintings in a gallery. 56 are sent to be cleaned. How many paintings remain? 28

10. Put these fractions in order, smallest first: $\frac{1}{2}$ $\frac{2}{3}$ $\frac{1}{3}$ $\frac{2}{3}$ $\frac{1}{2}$ $\frac{1}{3}$

11. 3 kg − 285 g = [2715] g

12. Share 54p and 76p equally between 2 children. How much does each child get? 65p

13. A radio station plays 8 commercials an hour. How many will it play in 9 hours? 72

14. If 1st December is on a Friday, what day is December 18th? Monday

15. What is the perimeter of this shape? 22 cm   (2 cm, 9 cm)

Exercise 14

A

1. £7·30 + £3·45 = £10·75
2. 82 + 13 = 95
3. 32 ÷ 8 = 4
4. 24 + 9 = 33
5. 42 − 7 = 35
6. 3 × 7 = 21
7. 54 − 35 = 19
8. 825, 824, 823, 822
9. 0·75 = 75%
10. 7 × 6 = 42 or 6 × 7
11. 48 + 8 + 5 = 61
12. (5 × 2) − 6 = 4
13. $\frac{1}{3}$ of 27 = 9
14. −25 −22 −19 −16
15. 972, 969, 966, 963

Copy and complete
the Decimal Function Machine
add 0·2

in	out
37·2	37·4
4·6	4·8
7·5	7·7
9·2	9·4
15·4	15·6
1·7	1·9
28·3	28·5
5·9	6·1
19·1	19·3

B

1. Put these numbers in order, smallest first: 4796, 647, 4976, 474   474, 647, 4796, 4976
2. Continue the pattern: 87, 80, 73, 66, 59
3. Round 18 295 to the nearest 1000.   18 000
4. Twenty-two plus seventy-seven = ninety-nine
5. How many odd numbers are there between 42 and 68?   13
6. 19 + 9 = 28
7. 4^2 − 9 = 7
8. Sixty-one children visited the farm on Monday and eighty-four on Thursday. How many children visited the farm altogether? one hundred and forty-five
9. How many 9 cm lengths can be cut from a ribbon 54 cm long?   6
10. 2, 10, 4, 1, 20, 5 are factors of which number?   20
11. $\frac{2}{3} = \frac{4}{6}$
12. What is the change from £5·00 if I spend £3·65?   £1·35
13. How many oranges at 21p each can I buy with £1·00?   4
14. Draw a rhombus.
15. The clock shows 20 past 7 but it is 35 minutes fast. What is the correct time? 6·45 or $\frac{1}{4}$ to 7

C

1. 3 × [4] = 12
2. £7·45 − £3·24 = £4·21
3. [24] ÷ 6 = 4
4. 67 + [11] = 78
5. 3498, 3499, [3500], 3501
6. £2·13 × 3 = £6·39
7. 13 ÷ 2 = 6 r [1]
8. 92 − 5 − [7] = 80
9. 641 + 237 = 878
10. (63 ÷ 7) − 1 = 8
11. 50% of [100] = 50
12. 591, [600], 609, 618
13. 17p + 48p = 65p
14. 9 + 3 + 8 + 14 = 34
15. 16 [+] 18 = 34

Copy and fill in the missing numbers.

```
  9 [7] 1 3
+ 4 0 8 [8]
-----------
  1 3 8 0 1
```

D

1. Write forty-four thousand four hundred and forty-four as a number. 44 444
2. 5 × 4 × 10 = 200
3. Imagine a 0 to 99 number square. Which number is one square to the left of 17? 16
4. Which number is not a multiple of 3? 33, 32, 42, 39, 36? 32
5. Two numbers multiplied together make 32. If one of them is 8, what is the other? 4
6. What is the sum of seventy-two and seventy-nine? one hundred and fifty-one
7. Estimate 716 + 246 to the nearest ten. 960
8. $\frac{1}{10}$ of 200 = 20
9. 92 people wanted to go skiing. There were only 78 places. How many people couldn't go? 14
10. Put these fractions in order, smallest first: $\frac{3}{4}$ $\frac{1}{2}$ $\frac{1}{3}$ $\frac{1}{3}$ $\frac{1}{2}$ $\frac{3}{4}$
11. 3·2 m + 95 cm = [415] cm
12. Share 19p and 35p equally between 2 children. How much does each child get? 27p
13. A train carriage holds 48 people. How many people are there in 3 carriages? 144
14. If 2nd February is a Thursday, what day is 9th February? Thursday
15. What is the perimeter of this shape? 28 cm   (7 cm × 7 cm square)

Exercise 15

A

1. £8·20 + £1·74 = £9·94
2. 54 + 28 = 82
3. [49] ÷ 7 = 7
4. 37 + [7] = 44
5. [72] − 8 = 64
6. 7 × [4] = 28
7. 43 − 24 = 19
8. 350, [349], 348, 347
9. 25% = [1]/[4]
10. [5] × [6] = 30 or others
11. 63 + 9 + 5 = 77
12. (7 × 2) − 2 = 12
13. $\frac{1}{6}$ of 48 = 8
14. −27 −22 [−17] −12
15. [432], 428, 424, 420

Use squared paper to plot the co-ordinates, then connect them in order.
(−6,2) (−4,4) (−2,2) (0,4) (−2,6)
(−4,4) (−6,6)

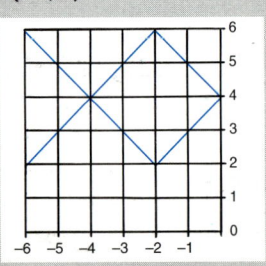

B

1. Put these numbers in order, smallest first: 1300, 103, 1030, 130   103, 130, 1030, 1300
2. Continue the pattern: 48, 60, 72, [84], [96]
3. Round 72 398 to the nearest 1000.   72 000
4. Twenty-seven plus sixty-two = eighty-nine
5. How many even numbers are there between 39 and 61?   11
6. 7[5] + 7 = 82
7. 7^2 + 6 = 55
8. On Valentine's day, the florist received 79 orders for carnations and 83 for roses. How many orders were received altogether?   162
9. 63 days make how many weeks?   9
10. 8, 1, 4, 2, are factors of which number?   8
11. $\frac{6}{8} = \frac{[3]}{4}$
12. What change do I get from £5·00 if I spend £3·88?   £1·12
13. How many apples at 13p each can I buy with £1·00?   7
14. Draw a regular pentagon.
15. It is $\frac{1}{4}$ to 2 on the clock. The clock is 10 minutes slow. What is the correct time?   5 to 2 or 1·55

C

1. 5 × [4] = 20
2. £9·27 − £6·15 = £3·12
3. [16] ÷ 2 = 8
4. 21 + [53] = 74
5. [2301], 2302, 2303, 2304
6. £1·22 × 4 = £4·88
7. 21 ÷ 4 = 5 r [1]
8. 86 − 9 − [4] = 73
9. 528 + 131 = 659
10. (40 ÷ 4) − 3 = 7
11. 25% of [200] = 50
12. [498], 503, 508, 513
13. 58p + 27p = 85p
14. 6 + 7 + 2 + 19 = 34
15. 98 [−] 27 = 71

Can you make 89 using any of the four operations and some or all of these numbers?

7	2
	27
53	
	39

D

1. Write fifty-three thousand, seven hundred as a number. 53 700
2. 3 × 3 × 4 = 36
3. Imagine a 0 to 99 number square. Which number is 2 squares below 11? 31
4. Which number is not a multiple of 5? 150, 170, 175, 155, 152? 152
5. Two numbers multiplied together make 54. If one of them is 6, what is the other? 9
6. What is the sum of eighty-one and fifty-seven? one hundred and thirty-eight
7. Estimate 337 + 886 to the nearest ten. 1220
8. $\frac{1}{4}$ of 80 = 20
9. A family set off on a 92 km journey. They stopped for petrol after 45 km. How many more km do they still have to travel? 47 km
10. Put these fractions in order, smallest first: $\frac{2}{3}$ $\frac{1}{6}$ $\frac{1}{3}$ $\frac{1}{6}$ $\frac{1}{3}$ $\frac{2}{3}$
11. 3·4 litres + 820 ml = [4220] ml
12. Share 48p and 32p equally between 2 children. How much does each child get? 40p
13. A baker can decorate 25 cakes in 1 hour. How many cakes can she decorate in 3 hours? 75
14. If 23rd November is a Friday, what day is 30th November. Friday
15. What is the perimeter of this shape? 22 cm   (3 cm, 8 cm)

Exercise 16

A

1. £5·50 + £3·27 = £8·77
2. 37 + 29 = 66
3. [28] ÷ 4 = 7
4. 34 + [9] = 43
5. [52] − 7 = 45
6. 7 × [8] = 56
7. 47 − 28 = 19
8. 142, 141, 140, [139]
9. 0·25 = [25]%
10. [7] × [2] = 14 or 2 × 7
11. 72 + 8 + 5 = 85
12. (8 × 7) − 7 = 49
13. $\frac{1}{2}$ of 20 = 10
14. [−28] −25 −22 −19
15. 634, [629], 624, 619

Copy and complete.

−	12	14	15	13
15	3	1	0	2
20	8	6	5	7
19	7	5	4	6
16	4	2	1	3

B

1. Put these numbers in order, smallest first:
   3625, 365, 362, 3562   362, 365, 3562, 3625
2. Continue the pattern: 120, 105, 90, [75], [60]
3. Round 42 199 to the nearest 1000.   42 000
4. Nineteen plus forty-six = sixty-five
5. How many odd numbers are there between 38 and 64?   13
6. 9[6] + 5 = 101
7. $6^2 − 9 = 25$
8. There are 46 children in year 4 and 67 children in year 5.
   How many children are there altogether?   113
9. Each minibus carries 11 passengers.
   How many minibuses are needed to transport 99 passengers?   9
10. 2, 16, 1, 8, 4 are factors of which number?   16
11. $\frac{1}{2} = \frac{[3]}{6}$
12. What is my change from £5·00 after I have spent £3·17?   £1·83
13. How many packets of crisps at 24p each can I buy with £1·00?   4
14. Draw a parallelogram.
15. The clock says 5 past 3, but it is 10 minutes slow. What is the correct time?
    quarter past 3 or 3·15

C

1. $7 \times \boxed{9} = 63$
2. £5·29 − £2·17 = £3·12
3. $\boxed{54} \div 6 = 9$
4. $53 + \boxed{26} = 79$
5. 1299, $\boxed{1300}$, 1301, 1302
6. £4·23 × 2 = £8·46
7. 30 ÷ 4 = 7 r $\boxed{2}$
8. 35 − 8 − $\boxed{4}$ = 23
9. 843 + 134 = 977
10. (81 ÷ 9) − 7 = 2
11. 50% of $\boxed{800}$ = 400
12. 737, 745, $\boxed{753}$, 761
13. 28p + 58p = 86p
14. 3 + 17 + 6 + 5 = 31
15. $9 \boxed{\div} 3 = 3$

How many ways can you make $2\frac{3}{5}$? Here is one example.

$1\frac{2}{5} + 1\frac{1}{5} = 2\frac{3}{5}$

D

1. Write sixty-eight thousand and seventy-six as a number. 68 076
2. 7 × 2 × 3 = 42
3. Imagine a 0 to 99 number square. Which number is 3 squares above 87? 57
4. Which number is not a multiple of 9? 72, 49, 27, 63, 81   49
5. Two numbers multiplied together make 42. If one of them is 7, what is the other? 6
6. What is the sum of twenty-five and ninety-six? 121
7. Estimate 772 + 596 to the nearest ten. 1370
8. $\frac{1}{5}$ of 50 = 10
9. A charity advertised for 68 volunteers. 81 people applied. How many more people applied than were needed? 13
10. Put these fractions in order, smallest first:
    $\frac{3}{10}$ $\frac{1}{2}$ $\frac{1}{5}$ $\frac{1}{5}$ $\frac{3}{10}$ $\frac{1}{2}$
11. 8·25 kg + 980 g = $\boxed{9}$ kg $\boxed{230}$ g
12. Share 63p and 21p equally between 2 children. How much does each child get? 42p
13. At a boarding school, 12 children sleep in each dormitory. How many children sleep in 5 dormitories? 60
14. If 17th October is a Thursday, what day is 27th October? Sunday
15. What is the perimeter of this shape? 40 cm   (10 cm × 10 cm square)

Exercise 17

A

1. £6·80 + £1·16 = £7·96
2. 26 + 18 = 44
3. 45 ÷ [9] = 5
4. [7] + 43 = 50
5. 62 − [9] = 53
6. [6] × 8 = 48
7. 52 − 36 = 16
8. 350, [349], 348, 347
9. 0·75 = [3]/[4]
10. [9] × [3] = 27 or 3 × 9
11. 85 + 6 + 3 = 94
12. (10 × 3) − 9 = 21
13. $\frac{1}{4}$ of 48 = 12
14. −18 −16 [−14] −12
15. [718], 712, 706, 700

Copy and complete the Decimal Function Machine
subtract 3·25

in	out
4·75	1·5
8	4·75
5	1·75
9·25	6
7·45	4·2
3·8	0·55
4·6	1·35
5·8	2·55
6	2·75

B

1. Put these numbers in order, smallest first:
   1685, 685, 6815, 586   586, 685, 1685, 6815
2. Continue the pattern:
   836, 842, 848, [854], [860]
3. Round 49 911 to the nearest 1000.   50 000
4. Forty-five plus thirty-seven = eighty-two
5. How many even numbers are there between 43 and 67?   12
6. 8[7] + 7 = 94
7. 8^2 + 7 = 71
8. Last week the rainfall was 24 mm and this week it was 59 mm. How much rain has fallen altogether?   83 mm
9. How many packets of 6 chocolate biscuits can be made up from 48 biscuits?   8
10. 3, 1, 24, 8, 2, 12, 4, 6, are all factors of which number?   24
11. $\frac{5}{10} = \frac{[1]}{2}$
12. What change do I get from £5·00 after spending £2·89?   £2·11
13. How many notebooks at 36p each can I buy for £1·00?   2
14. Draw a trapezium.
15. If the clock shows 25 to 1, but the clock is 15 minutes slow, what is the correct time?
    10 to 1 or 12·50

C

1. 8 × ⟨7⟩ = 56
2. £7·73 − £4·31 = £3·42
3. ⟨18⟩ ÷ 9 = 2
4. 35 + ⟨23⟩ = 58
5. ⟨3000⟩, 3001, 3002, 3003
6. £2·31 × 3 = £6·93
7. 38 ÷ 5 = 7 r ⟨3⟩
8. 43 − 6 − ⟨5⟩ = 32
9. 235 + 564 = 799
10. (27 ÷ 3) − 2 = 7
11. 25% of ⟨800⟩ = 200
12. ⟨246⟩, 254, 262, 270
13. 19p + 27p = 46p
14. 8 + 5 + 14 + 2 = 29
15. 85 ⟨−⟩ 37 = 48

Copy and fill in the missing numbers.

```
   2 7 3 5
 − 1 ⟨6⟩ 4 7
   -------
   1 0 8 8
```

D

1. Write fifty-three thousand, eight hundred and fourteen as a number.   53 814
2. 6 × 3 × 3 = 54
3. Imagine a 0 to 99 number square. Which number is 2 squares to the left of 46?   44
4. Which number is not a multiple of 8? 88, 16, 34, 56, 72?   34
5. Two numbers multiplied together make 48. If one of them is 6, what is the other?   8
6. What is the sum of fifty-seven and seventy-five?   one hundred and thirty-two
7. Estimate 547 + 639 to the nearest ten.   1190
8. $\frac{1}{3}$ of 99 = 33
9. 32 people want tickets for a play, but there are only 18 seats left. How many people do not get a seat?   14
10. Put these fractions in order, smallest first:
    $\frac{1}{2}$ $\frac{2}{5}$ $\frac{1}{4}$ $\frac{1}{4}$ $\frac{2}{5}$ $\frac{1}{2}$
11. 2 km − 80 m = ⟨1920⟩ m
12. Share 22p and 43p equally among 5 children. How much does each child get?   13p
13. Pauline buys four dozen eggs. How many eggs is this?   48
14. If 31st May is a Sunday, what day is 5th June?   Friday
15. What is the perimeter of this shape?   28 cm

6 cm
8 cm

Exercise 18

A

1. £1·40 + £1·53 = £2·93
2. 45 + 46 = 91
3. [72] ÷ 9 = 8
4. 79 + [7] = 86
5. [80] – 6 = 74
6. 9 × [3] = 27
7. 29 – 18 = 11
8. 725, 724, [723], 722
9. 0·5 = [50]%
10. [7] × [3] = 21 or 3 × 7
11. 41 + 7 + 4 = 52
12. (2 × 4) – 8 = 0
13. $\frac{1}{5}$ of 45 = 9
14. –32 [–29] –26 –23
15. 758, 752, [746], 740

Use squared paper to plot the co-ordinates, then connect them in order.
(0,3) (–1,6) (–2,3) (–3,6) (–4,3) (–5,6) (–6,3) (–5,0) (–4,3) (–3,0) (–2,3) (–1,0) (0,3)

B

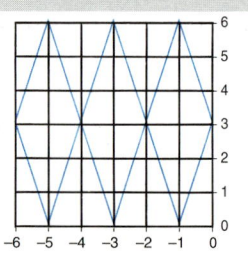

1. Put these numbers in order, smallest first:
   1002, 201, 2001, 102   102, 201, 1002, 2001
2. Continue the pattern:
   756, 749, 742, [735], [728]
3. Round 55 496 to the nearest 1000.   55 000
4. thirty-five plus sixty-nine = one hundred and four
5. How many odd numbers are there between 46 and 72?   13
6. 6[3] + 8 = 71
7. 10^2 – 9 = 91
8. On the first day of the sale, 88 mugs were sold. On the second day 18 more were sold.
   What was the total sold? 106
9. 72 fibre-tip pens can be sorted into how many packs of 8 each?   9
10. 7, 1, 21, 3, are factors of which number? 21
11. $\frac{[2]}{10} = \frac{1}{5}$
12. What change from £5·00 would I get after spending £2·41   £2·59
13. How many lollipops at 11p each can I buy for £2·12?   19
14. I am a regular four-sided shape. My sides are all the same length and I have 4 right angles. What am I?   a square
15. A clock shows $\frac{1}{4}$ past 4. If this clock is 10 minutes fast, what time is the correct time?   5 past 4 or 4·05

C

1. 6 × [6] = 36
2. £8·34 − £5·12 = £3·22
3. [20] ÷ 4 = 5
4. 23 + [41] = 64
5. 4258, 4259, [4260], 4261
6. £2·12 × 4 = £8·48
7. 17 ÷ 2 = 8 r [1]
8. 72 − 7 − [8] = 57
9. 451 + 443 = 894
10. (56 ÷ 8) − 6 = 1
11. 50% of [300] = 150
12. 652, 752, [852], 952
13. 32p + 48p = 80p
14. 8 + 7 + 15 + 1 = 31
15. 8 [×] 4 = 32

Can you make 121 using any of the four operations and some or all of these numbers?

6, 3, 41, 19, 62

D

1. Write seventy-six thousand and nine as a number. 76 009
2. 8 × 5 × 4 = 160
3. Imagine a 0 to 99 number square. Which number is 3 squares above 68? 38
4. Which number is not a multiple of 7? 77, 44, 14, 63, 35   44
5. Two numbers multiplied together make 63. If one of them is 9, what is the other? 7
6. What is the sum of eighty-eight and ninety-nine? one hundred and eighty-seven
7. Estimate 314 + 468 to the nearest ten. 780
8. $\frac{1}{6}$ of 30 = 5
9. Dean baked 65 cakes for the school fair. At the end only 17 cakes remained. How many were sold? 48
10. Put these fractions in order, smallest first:
    $\frac{2}{7}$ $\frac{1}{6}$ $\frac{1}{8}$ $\frac{1}{8}$ $\frac{1}{6}$ $\frac{2}{7}$
11. 3·6 km + 270 m = [3870] m
12. Share 81p and 19p equally among 5 children. How much does each child get? 20p
13. A shop sells an average of 15 cans of drink every day. How many cans will be sold in 5 days? 75
14. If 28th February is a Tuesday, what day is 6th March? Monday
15. What is the perimeter of this shape? 42 cm (9 cm, 12 cm)

Exercise 19

A

1. £4·20 + £4·16 = £8·36
2. 34 + 67 = 101
3. 24 ÷ [8] = 3
4. [6] + 63 = 69
5. 97 − [9] = 88
6. [3] × 6 = 18
7. 35 − 26 = 9
8. 461, 460, [459], 458
9. 50% = $\frac{1}{2}$
10. [5] × [9] = 45 or 9 × 5
11. 43 + 5 + 9 = 57
12. (7 × 6) − 8 = 34
13. $\frac{1}{3}$ of 21 = 7
14. [−31] −28 −25 −22
15. 217, 209, 201, [193]

Copy and complete.

×	9	11	6	12
7	63	77	42	84
12	108	121	72	144
8	72	88	48	96
9	81	99	54	108

B

1. Put these numbers in order, smallest first:
3730, 3037, 3370, 370   370, 3037, 3370, 3730
2. Continue the pattern:
532, 543, 554, [565], [576]
3. Round 73 294 to the nearest 1000.   73 000
4. Twenty-six plus sixty-six = ninety-two
5. How many even numbers are there between 67 and 95?   14
6. 5[2] + 9 = 61
7. 9² + 9 = 90
8. In a maths test Jack got 53 marks on one paper and 84 marks on another. What were his marks in total?   137
9. How many taxis each holding 4 passengers will be needed to transport 36 people to the station?   9
10. 6, 5, 10, 30, 3, 1, are factors of which number?   30
11. $\frac{4}{8} = \frac{1}{2}$
12. What change from £5·00 do I get after spending £1·72?   £3·28
13. How many 29p ice-creams can I buy for £1·00?   3
14. I am a four-sided shape with four right angles. Two of my sides are longer than the other two. What am I?   a rectangle / an oblong
15. It is 10 to 10 on a clock that is 10 minutes slow. What is the correct time?
10 oclock or 10·00

C

1. $4 \times \boxed{6} = 24$
2. £3·37 − £1·16 = £2·21
3. $\boxed{21} \div 7 = 3$
4. $42 + \boxed{35} = 77$
5. $\boxed{4999}$, 5000, 5001, 5002
6. £1·32 × 3 = £3·96
7. $23 \div 3 = 7 \text{ r } \boxed{2}$
8. $53 - 4 - \boxed{7} = 42$
9. 161 + 326 = 487
10. (36 ÷ 6) − 4 = 2
11. 25% of $\boxed{800}$ = 200
12. $\boxed{198}$, 206, 214, 222
13. 46p + 29p = 75p
14. 13 + 3 + 4 + 7 = 27
15. $42 \boxed{+} 19 = 61$

How many ways can you make $1\tfrac{1}{5}$? Here is one example.

$\tfrac{2}{5} + \tfrac{4}{5} = 1\tfrac{1}{5}$

D

1. Write eighty-nine thousand, seven hundred and twelve as a number.   89 712
2. $7 \times 7 \times 2 =$ 98
3. Imagine a 0 to 99 number square. Which number is 3 squares to the left of 39?   36
4. Which number is not a multiple of 6? 62, 36, 72, 24, 54?   62
5. Two numbers multiplied together make 64. If one of them is 8, what is the other?   8
6. What is the sum of thirty-seven and eighty-seven?   124
7. Estimate 875 + 578 to the nearest ten.   1450
8. $\tfrac{1}{5}$ of 150 = 30
9. 87 children are in the school dining hall. If 49 have school dinners, how many have packed lunches?   38
10. Put these fractions in order, largest first:
    $\tfrac{4}{6}$ $\tfrac{1}{3}$ $\tfrac{2}{9}$ $\tfrac{4}{6}$ $\tfrac{1}{3}$ $\tfrac{2}{9}$
11. 5 kg − 265 g = $\boxed{4735}$ g
12. Share 16p and 32p equally among four children. How much does each child get?   12p
13. In a big box of chocolates there are 17 on each layer. If there are 3 layers, how many chocolates are there altogether?   51
14. If 7th May is a Wednesday, what day is 20th May?   Tuesday
15. What is the perimeter of this shape?   26 cm   6 cm   7 cm

Exercise 20

A

1. £2·30 + £5·28 = £7·58
2. 53 + 39 = 92
3. ☐15☐ ÷ 3 = 5
4. 87 + ☐6☐ = 93
5. ☐35☐ − 6 = 29
6. 4 × ☐3☐ = 12
7. 81 − 72 = 9
8. ☐660☐, 659, 658, 657
9. 0·33 = ☐1☐/3
10. ☐7☐ × ☐8☐ = 56 or 8 × 7
11. 75 + 6 + 8 = 89
12. (8 × 3) − 4 = 20
13. $\frac{1}{6}$ of 54 = 9
14. −45 ☐−40☐ −35 −30
15. 873, 867, 861, ☐855☐

Copy and complete the Decimal Function Machine
add 1·3

in	out
16·6	17·9
15·2	16·5
32·2	33·5
51·5	52·8
14·3	15·6
27·1	28·4
46·4	47·7
19·5	20·8
93·3	94·6

B

1. Put these numbers in order, smallest first:
7895, 7985, 759, 7958   759, 7895, 7958, 7985

2. Continue the pattern:
444, 436, 428, ☐420☐, ☐412☐

3. Round 95 469 to the nearest 1000.   95 000

4. Eighty-six add seventeen = one hundred and three

5. How many odd numbers are there between 88 and 106?   9

6. 4☐4☐ + 8 = 52

7. 8^2 − 9 = 55

8. Class 5 got 96 Easter eggs between them and Class 6 got 77 between them. What is the sum of the 2 classes' Easter eggs?   173

9. How many packets of 3 pens each can I fill if I have 27 pens?   9

10. 36, 12, 1, 3, 6, 18, 2, are factors of which number?   36

11. $\frac{6}{10}$ = ☐3☐/5

12. What change from £5·00 do I get if I spend 63p?   £4·37

13. How many chocolate biscuits at 19p each can I buy for £1·00?   5

14. I am a four-sided shape. 2 of my sides are parallel, although one is shorter than the other. My other 2 sides are not parallel. What am I?   a trapezium

15. It is 20 past 8 on a clock that is 25 minutes fast. What is the correct time?   5 to 8 or 7·55

C

1. $2 \times \boxed{9} = 18$
2. £5·93 − £2·51 = £3·42
3. $\boxed{40} \div 8 = 5$
4. $34 + \boxed{31} = 65$
5. 2519, 2520, $\boxed{2521}$, 2522
6. £4·12 × 2 = £8·24
7. 35 ÷ 4 = 8 r $\boxed{3}$
8. $75 - 8 - \boxed{6} = 61$
9. 729 + 211 = 940
10. (22 ÷ 2) − 1 = 10
11. 50% of $\boxed{50}$ = 25
12. 127, 137, 147, $\boxed{157}$
13. 57p + 35p = 92p
14. 2 + 18 + 6 + 4 = 30
15. $56 \boxed{\div} 8 = 7$

Copy and fill in the missing numbers.

$$3\;8\;\boxed{4}\;2 \\ \times \quad\quad 6 \\ \overline{2\;\boxed{3}\;0\;5\;2}$$

D

1. Write ninety-six thousand as a number. 96 000
2. 3 × 5 × 3 = 45
3. Imagine a 0 to 99 number square. Which number is 4 squares to the right of 72? 76
4. Which number is not a multiple of 3? 60, 51, 66, 46, 42   46
5. Two numbers multiplied together make 56. If one of them is 7, what is the other? 8
6. What is the sum of fifty-four and seventy-eight? one hundred and thirty-two
7. Estimate 679 + 488 to the nearest ten.   1170
8. $\frac{1}{8}$ of 160 = 20
9. Ross has collected 37 stickers. If there are 81 stickers in the whole collection, how many more does he need? 44
10. Put these fractions in order, smallest first: $\frac{3}{4}\quad\frac{11}{12}\quad\frac{9}{10}$ $\frac{3}{4}\quad\frac{9}{10}\quad\frac{11}{12}$
11. 4 km 620 m + 590 m = $\boxed{5210}$ m
12. Share 36p and 18p equally among 3 children. How much does each child get? 18p
13. Judy picked enough apples to fill 5 boxes. Each box holds 19 apples. How many apples has she picked? 95
14. If 30th September is a Tuesday, what day is 8th October. Wednesday
15. What is the perimeter of this shape? 42 cm (5 cm, 16 cm)

Exercise 21

A

1. £2·73 + £2·19 = £4·92
2. 47 + 29 = 76
3. [24] ÷ 2 = 12
4. 13 + [13] = 26
5. 73 − [21] = 52
6. [8] × 2 = 16
7. 57 − [9] = 48
8. 1264, 1265, 1266, [1267]
9. $\frac{1}{2}$ of 100 = 50
10. 57 + 6 − 3 = 60
11. (4 × 6) + 12 = 36
12. 279 − 46 = 233
13. 123 × 2 = 246
14. −8 −4 [0] 4
15. 3768, 3775, 3782, [3789]

Use squared paper to plot the co-ordinates, then connect them in order.

(0,−1) (−1,−3) (−2,−2) (−3,−3)
(−4,−2) (−5,−3) (−6,−1) (−6,−6)
(−5,−4) (−4,−5) (−3,−4) (−2,−5)
(−1,−4) (0,−6) (0,−1)

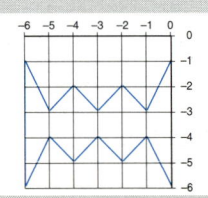

B

1. Round 2766 to the nearest 10. 2770
2. Put these numbers in order, smallest first:
   56 413, 56 431, 56 341, 56 314
   56 314, 56 341, 56 413, 56 431
3. In the number 6795, which digit tells us how many 10s there are? 9
4. Eighty-five subtract sixty-two = twenty-three
5. How many odd numbers are there between 272 and 284? 6
6. [4]6 − 4 = 42
7. 3^2 + 12 = 21
8. Simon had 76 football stickers. He gave 24 away. How many did he have left? 52
9. There are 6 eggs in a box. How many eggs in 7 boxes? 42
10. 27, 54, 81 are multiples of which number? 9
11. Which is larger, 0·5 or $\frac{1}{3}$? 0·5
12. Are these lines parallel? yes 
13. Write the co-ordinates. (6,4) 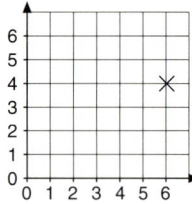
14. What is my change from £2·00 after I have spent £1·60 and 32p? 8p
15. How much time has passed?
    2h 15 min or $2\frac{1}{4}$ hours

C

1. $\boxed{5} \times 7 = 35$
2. £6·33 − £4·28 = £2·05
3. 27 ÷ $\boxed{9}$ = 3
4. $\boxed{28}$ + 17 = 45
5. 3658, 3657, $\boxed{3656}$, 3655
6. £1·17 × 3 = £3·51
7. 19 ÷ 5 = $\boxed{3}$ r $\boxed{4}$
8. $\boxed{54}$ − 7 − 8 = 39
9. 316 + 27 = 343
10. (20 ÷ 10) + 12 = 14
11. 0·2 × 30 = 6
12. 4321, 4317, 4313, $\boxed{4309}$
13. 58p + 69p = £1·27
14. 8 + 9 + 7 + 65 = 89
15. 85 $\boxed{-}$ 16 = 69

Can you make 829 using any of the four operations and some or all of these numbers?

5, 8, 71, 32, 53

D

1. Write two hundred and seventy-one thousand, three hundred and eighty-nine as a number. 271 389
2. (3 × 4) ÷ 6 = 2
3. Imagine a 0 to 99 number square. Which 2 numbers are diagonally above 45? 34 and 36
4. Write the next multiple of 9: 72, 81, 90, 99
5. Two numbers multiplied together make 56. If one of them is 4, what is the other? 14
6. What is the difference between seventy-two and forty-eight? twenty-four
7. Estimate 432 − 297 to the nearest ten. 130
8. $\frac{2}{3}$ of 90 = 60
9. If there are 29 children in one class and 28 in another, how many children are there altogether? 57
10. Which is smaller, $\frac{1}{3}$ or 25%? 25%
11. 3 m − 14 cm − 5 cm = $\boxed{281}$ cm
12. If a teacher divides 35 children into 7 teams, how many children are there in each team? 5
13. Matty spent 0·25 of his pocket money. Write what is left as a fraction. $\frac{3}{4}$
14. If each square represents 1 cm², what is the area of this shape? $\boxed{55}$ cm²
15. Start: 12:10   Finish: a.m.   How much time has passed? 5h 5 mins

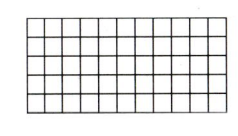

Exercise 22

A

1. £4·69 + £2·13 = £6·82
2. 58 + 37 = 95
3. 90 ÷ 10 = 9
4. 12 + 24 = 36
5. 65 − 41 = 24
6. 7 × 6 = 42
7. 63 − 7 = 56
8. 3472, 3473, 3474, 3475
9. $\frac{1}{4}$ of 100 = 25
10. 43 + 8 − 4 = 47
11. (3 × 9) + 11 = 38
12. 362 − 41 = 321
13. 221 × 3 = 663
14. −7 −2 3 8
15. 4597, 4605, 4613, 4621

Copy and complete.

÷	10	2	5	1
50	5	25	10	50
20	2	10	4	20
110	11	55	22	110
90	9	45	18	90

B

1. Round 4593 to the nearest 10.   4590
2. Put these numbers in order, smallest first:
   36 315, 36 415, 36 135, 36 351
   36 135, 36 315, 36 351, 36 415
3. In the number 3478 which digit tells us how many 10s there are?   7
4. Forty-seven subtract twenty-three = twenty-four
5. How many odd numbers are there between 674 and 688?   7
6. 3 9 − 5 = 34
7. 2^2 + 16 = 20
8. John buys a chocolate bar for 53p. He gives the shop owner 70p. How much change does he receive?   17p
9. How many fingers and thumbs do 4 people have altogether?   40
10. 42, 48, 72 are multiples of which number?   6
11. Which is larger, $\frac{1}{2}$ $\frac{1}{5}$ $\frac{1}{3}$? $\frac{1}{2}$
12. Are these lines parallel?   yes
13. Write the co-ordinates.   (1,5)
14. What is my change from £2·00 after I have spent £1·20 and 46p?   34p
15. How much time has passed?
    2h 15min or $2\frac{1}{4}$ hours

C

1. $\boxed{4} \times 4 = 16$
2. £7·45 − £3·37 = £4·08
3. 48 ÷ $\boxed{8}$ = 6
4. $\boxed{17}$ + 16 = 33
5. 4220, $\boxed{4219}$, 4218, 4217
6. £1·19 × 6 = £7·14
7. 29 ÷ 4 = $\boxed{7}$ r $\boxed{1}$
8. $\boxed{38}$ − 6 − 5 = 27
9. 417 + 45 = 462
10. (32 ÷ 4) + 14 = 22
11. 0·5 × 50 = 25
12. 8721, 8715, $\boxed{8709}$, 8703
13. 27p + 85p = £1·12
14. 5 + 6 + 9 + 61 = 81
15. 18 $\boxed{+}$ 65 = 83

How many ways can you make $3\frac{2}{3}$? Here is one example.

$2 + 1\frac{2}{3} = 3\frac{2}{3}$

D

1. Write seven hundred and twenty-nine thousand, two hundred and ninety-four as a number. 729 294
2. (6 × 2) ÷ 4 = 3
3. Imagine a 0 to 99 number square. Which 2 numbers are diagonally below 63? 72 and 74
4. Write the next multiple of 7: 77, 84, 91, $\boxed{98}$
5. Two numbers multiplied together make 96. If one of them is 6, what is the other? 16
6. What is the difference between sixty-one and forty-nine? twelve
7. Estimate 569 − 233 to the nearest ten. 340
8. $\frac{3}{5}$ of 100 = 60
9. There are 16 children in the team already. How many more are needed to make it up to 25? 9
10. Which is smaller, $\frac{1}{4}$ or 0·3? $\frac{1}{4}$
11. 4 kg − 200 g − 70 g = $\boxed{3730}$ g
12. A bookcase holds 54 books. If there are 6 shelves, how many books are there on each shelf? 9
13. Michael lost $\frac{1}{3}$ of his pocket money. What fraction is left? $\frac{2}{3}$
14. If each square represents 1 cm², what is the area of this shape? $\boxed{30}$ cm²
15. Start: 07:15 Finish: a.m.
How much time has passed?
4h 15 min or $4\frac{1}{4}$ hours

Exercise 23

A

1. £3·36 + £2·15 = £5·51
2. 29 + 68 = 97
3. 21 ÷ [3] = 7
4. [31] + 23 = 54
5. 54 − [41] = 13
6. [2] × 3 = 6
7. [45] − 8 = 37
8. 2677, 2678, 2679, [2680]
9. 0·5 × 100 = 50
10. 93 − 6 + 2 = 89
11. (2 × 4) + 19 = 27
12. 648 − 33 = 615
13. 121 × 4 = 484
14. −12 −3 6 [15]
15. 5384, [5391], 5398, 5405

Copy and complete the Decimal Function Machine **subtract 0·5**

in	out
8·2	7·7
7·8	7·3
2	1·5
6·25	5·75
1	0·5
3·5	3
5	4·5
4·75	4·25
9·65	9·15

B

1. Round 3462 to the nearest 10. 3460
2. Put these numbers in order, smallest first: 40 635, 40 365, 40 563, 40 653
   40 365, 40 563, 40 635, 40 653
3. In the number 9154 which digit tells us how many 10s there are? 5
4. Fifty-six subtract forty-one = fifteen
5. How many even numbers are there between 351 and 367? 8
6. [9]7 − 2 = 95
7. 4² − 11 = 5
8. There are 46 counters on the table. If Melissa takes away 12 counters, how many are left? 34
9. What is seven multiplied by nine? 63
10. 25, 40, 65 are multiples of which number? 5
11. Which is larger, $\frac{1}{3}$ or $\frac{1}{5}$? $\frac{1}{3}$
12. Are these lines parallel? yes
13. Write the co-ordinates.
    (4,2)
14. What is my change from £2·00 after I have spent £1·10 and 57p? 33p
15. How much time has passed?
    1 hr 45 min or $1\frac{3}{4}$ hours

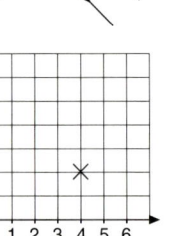

C

1. $\boxed{10} \times 3 = 30$
2. £6·52 − £2·48 = £4·04
3. $35 \div \boxed{7} = 5$
4. $\boxed{49} + 19 = 68$
5. 8749, 8748, 8747, $\boxed{8746}$
6. £1·12 × 4 = £4·48
7. $46 \div 7 = \boxed{6}$ r $\boxed{4}$
8. $\boxed{66} - 3 - 9 = 54$
9. 935 + 27 = 962
10. (16 ÷ 8) + 11 = 13
11. 0·25 × 40 = 10
12. 5342, $\boxed{5335}$, 5328, 5321
13. 49p + 72p = £1·21
14. 3 + 8 + 7 + 47 = 65
15. $14 \boxed{\times} 3 = 42$

Copy and fill in the missing numbers.

1620 ÷ 3 $\boxed{6}$ = 45

D

1. Write one hundred and sixty-two thousand, five hundred and thirteen as a number. 162 513
2. (5 × 8) ÷ 4 = 10
3. Imagine a 0 to 99 number square. Which 2 numbers are diagonally to the left of 52? 41 and 61
4. Write the next multiple of 3: 42, 45, 48, $\boxed{51}$
5. Two numbers multiplied together make 135. If one of them is 9, what is the other? 15
6. What is the difference between thirty-two and twenty-seven? five
7. Estimate 341 − 179 to the nearest ten. 160
8. $\frac{2}{5}$ of 55 is $\boxed{22}$
9. Fizel has 38 red counters and 27 blue counters. How many does he have altogether? 65
10. Which is smaller, $\frac{1}{3}$ or 0·5? $\frac{1}{3}$
11. 5 litres + 70 ml + 26 ml = $\boxed{5096}$ ml
12. A cyclist has to travel 72 km. If she travels 9 km every hour how many hours will it take her? 8
13. Toni and her friends ate 20% of a cake. Write what is left as a fraction. $\frac{4}{5}$
14. If each square represents 1 cm², what is the area of this shape $\boxed{30}$ cm²
15. Start: 13:30   Finish: a.m. How much time has passed? 3h 15 min or $3\frac{1}{4}$ hours

Exercise 24

A

1. £1·48 + £3·25 = £4·73
2. 34 + 39 = 73
3. 42 ÷ [7] = 6
4. [22] + 24 = 46
5. 88 − 23 = 65
6. 4 × [8] = 32
7. [92] − 7 = 85
8. 7948, 7949, [7950], 7951
9. 0·25 × 100 = 25
10. 38 + 7 − 2 = 43
11. (5 × 3) + 14 = 29
12. 566 − 25 = 541
13. 432 × 2 = 864
14. [−8] −3 2 7
15. 6987, 6995, [7003], 7011

Use squared paper to plot the co-ordinates, then connect them in order.
(−1,1) (−3,−4) (−5,−1) (−5,−4)
(−3,−1) (−1,−4) (−1,−1)

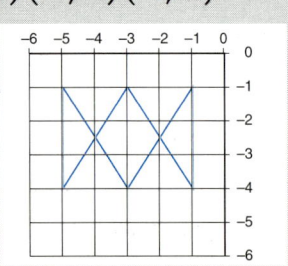

B

1. Round 7258 to the nearest 10. 7260
2. Put these numbers in order, smallest first:
   27 985, 27 892, 27 761, 27 634
   27 634, 27 761, 27 892, 27 985
3. In the number 1378 which digit tells us how many 100s there are? 3
4. Seventy-nine subtract fifty-eight. twenty-one
5. How many even numbers are there between 107 and 121? 7
6. [5]8 − 6 = 52
7. 6^2 − 14 = 22
8. Natasha buys a dress for £14·00 and pays with a £20·00 note. How much change does she get? £6·00
9. 7 children have 10p each. How much money do they have altogether? 70p
10. 24, 30, 36 are multiples of which number? 6
11. Which is larger, $\frac{1}{3}$ $\frac{1}{4}$ or $\frac{1}{5}$? $\frac{1}{3}$
12. Are these lines parallel? 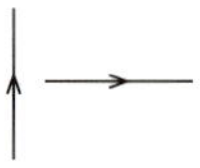 no
13. Write the co-ordinates.
    (2,3) 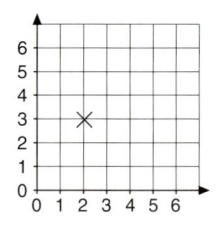
14. What is the change from £2·00 after I have spent £1·30 and 47p? 23p
15. How much time has passed?
    1h 45 min or $1\frac{3}{4}$ hours

C

1. $\boxed{3} \times 7 = 21$
2. £3·48 − £1·34 = £2·14
3. 49 ÷ $\boxed{7}$ = 7
4. $\boxed{19}$ + 18 = 37
5. 2658, 2657, $\boxed{2656}$, 2655
6. £1·16 × 5 = £5·80
7. 21 ÷ 6 = $\boxed{3}$ r $\boxed{3}$
8. $\boxed{51}$ − 7 − 6 = 38
9. 683 + 19 = 702
10. (25 ÷ 5) + 13 = 18
11. 0·2 × 50 = 10
12. $\boxed{3515}$, 3521, 3527, 3533
13. 87p + 45p = £1·32
14. 4 + 6 + 6 + 82 = 98
15. 5 $\boxed{÷}$ 1 = 5

Can you make 211 using any of the four operations and some or all of these numbers?

3, 4, 58, 21, 132

D

1. Write eight hundred and thirty-one thousand, one hundred and eight as a number. 831 108
2. (3 × 8) ÷ 6 = 4
3. Imagine a 0 to 99 number square. Which 2 numbers are diagonally to the right of 27? 18 and 38
4. Write the next multiple of 6: 96, 102, 108, $\boxed{114}$
5. Two numbers multiplied together make 126. If one of them is 7, what is the other? 18
6. What is the difference between ninety-seven and sixty-eight? twenty-nine
7. Estimate 732 − 632 to the nearest ten. 100
8. $\frac{3}{4}$ of 24 = 18
9. Ms Thomas needs 32 members for her maths club. 24 have said they will join. How many more are needed? 8
10. Which is larger, 20% or 0·25? 0·25
11. 73 cm + 8 m + 100 cm = $\boxed{973}$ cm
12. If each song lasts 3 minutes, how many songs can you fit on an hour's tape? 20
13. David ate 0·2 of a chocolate bar. Write what is left as a fraction. $\frac{4}{5}$
14. If each square represents 1 cm², what is the area of this shape? $\boxed{16}$ cm²
15. Start: 19:45 Finish: p.m.
    How much time has passed? 3·15 min or $3\frac{1}{4}$ hours

25% of 60

4620 × 7

684 ÷ ?

Exercise 25

A

1. £6·23 + £2·65 = £8·88
2. 18 + 67 = 85
3. 56 ÷ 7 = 8
4. 25 + 54 = 79
5. 56 − 24 = 32
6. 7 × 4 = 28
7. 43 − 9 = 34
8. 3724, 3725, 3726, 3727
9. $\frac{1}{5}$ of 100 = 20
10. 67 + 9 − 8 = 68
11. (7 × 6) + 11 = 53
12. 937 − 14 = 923
13. 312 × 3 = 936
14. −11 −5 1 7
15. 2010, 2018, 2026, 2034

Copy and complete.

+	57	29	42	38
25	82	54	67	63
32	89	61	74	70
46	103	75	88	84
68	125	97	110	106

B

1. Round 5017 to the nearest 10. 5020
2. Put these numbers in order, smallest first: 12 598, 12 458, 12 558, 12 568
   12 458, 12 558, 12 568, 12 598
3. In the number 5248 which digit tells us how many 100s there are? 2
4. Sixty-seven subtract forty-one = twenty-six
5. How many odd numbers are there between 436 and 448? 6
6. 64 − 1 = 63
7. 5^2 + 13 = 38
8. 84 children are in school. If 37 have packed lunch, how many have school dinners? 47
9. In a mini-bus each seat holds 2 children. How many are in a bus with 12 seats? 24
10. 35, 49, 63 are multiples of which number? 7
11. Which is larger, $\frac{1}{3}$ $\frac{1}{6}$ or $\frac{1}{5}$? $\frac{1}{3}$
12. Are these lines parallel? no
13. Write the co-ordinates. (3,5)
14. What is my change from £2·00 after I have spent £1·20 and 72p? 8p
15. How much time has passed? 2h 20 min

C

1. $\boxed{4} \times 6 = 24$
2. £4·28 − £2·16 = £2·12
3. 48 ÷ $\boxed{6}$ = 8
4. $\boxed{69}$ + 15 = 84
5. 7401, 7400, $\boxed{7499}$, 7498
6. £1·15 × 2 = £2·30
7. 28 ÷ 3 = $\boxed{9}$ r $\boxed{1}$
8. $\boxed{45}$ − 8 − 8 = 29
9. 245 + 27 = 272
10. (42 ÷ 6) + 19 = 26
11. 0·25 × 20 = 5
12. 4060, 4052, $\boxed{4044}$, 4036
13. 35p + 67p = £1·02
14. 64 + 8 + 7 + 9 = 88
15. 13 $\boxed{\times}$ 3 = 39

How many ways can you make $1\frac{1}{6}$? Here is one example.

$5 - 1\frac{2}{3} - 2\frac{1}{6} = 1\frac{1}{6}$

D

1. Write six hundred and forty-two thousand, two hundred and sixty-four as a number.   642 264
2. (4 × 6) ÷ 3 = 8
3. Imagine a 0 to 99 number square. Which numbers are diagonally above 78?   67 and 69
4. Write the next multiple of 8: 152, 160, 168, $\boxed{176}$
5. Two numbers multiplied together make 152. If one of them is 8, what is the other?   19
6. What is the difference between fifty-three and twenty-six.   twenty-seven
7. Estimate 698 − 421 to the nearest ten.   280
8. $\frac{1}{3}$ of 150 = 50
9. If you buy 79 g of cheese and 75 g of butter, what weight will you have to carry?   154 g
10. Which is larger, 0·2 or 33%?   33%
11. 6 m + 70 cm + 12 cm = $\boxed{682}$ cm
12. A box holds 56 oranges. If there are 7 layers, how many oranges are on each layer?   8
13. Alice and her family have travelled 0·5 of their journey. Write what is left as a fraction. $\frac{1}{2}$
14. If each square represents 1 cm², what is the area of this shape? $\boxed{24}$ cm²
15. Start: 04:20   Finish: a.m.
    How much time has passed?   2 h 50 min

25% of 60

4620 × 7

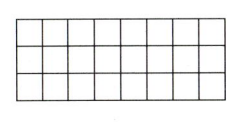

684 ÷ ?

Exercise 26

A

1. £8·24 + £1·37 = £9·61
2. 63 + 28 = 91
3. 54 ÷ 6 = 9
4. 23 + 34 = 57
5. 48 − 22 = 26
6. 8 × 8 = 64
7. 28 − 9 = 19
8. 5027, 5028, 5029, 5030
9. 20% of 100 = 20
10. 85 − 9 + 7 = 83
11. (8 × 3) + 15 = 39
12. 725 − 23 = 702
13. 423 × 2 = 846
14. −9 −2 5 12
15. 4016, 4020, 4024, 4028

Copy and complete the Decimal Function Machine
add 0·8

in	out
5·21	6·01
4·07	4·87
4·39	5·19
6·37	7·17
2·66	3·46
1·58	2·38
2·45	3·25
8·34	9·14
3·46	4·26

B

1. Round 8368 to the nearest 10. 8370
2. Put these numbers in order, smallest first: 86371, 84671, 83761, 83176
   83176, 83761, 84671, 86371
3. In the number 2034 which digit tells us how many 10s there are? 3
4. Thirty-seven subtract sixteen = twenty-one
5. How many even numbers are there between 531 and 543? 6
6. 7 7 − 5 = 72
7. 7^2 − 10 = 39
8. There are 36 red smarties in one bowl, and 27 blue smarties in another. How many more red smarties are there than blue smarties? 9
9. If seven apples are cut into quarters, how many pieces will there be? 28
10. 16, 32, 56 are multiples of which number? 8
11. Which is the larger, $\frac{1}{3}$ or $\frac{1}{6}$? $\frac{1}{3}$
12. Are these lines parallel? 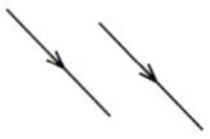 yes
13. Write the co-ordinates. (5,3) 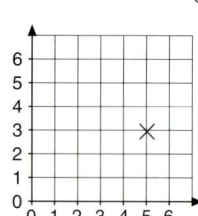
14. What is the change from £2·00 after I have spent £1·50 and 35p? 15p
15. How much time has passed? 2h 20 min

C

1. $\boxed{5} \times 8 = 40$
2. £9·27 − £7·16 = £2·11
3. 14 ÷ $\boxed{2}$ = 7
4. $\boxed{35}$ + 17 = 52
5. 5542, 5541, 5540, $\boxed{5539}$
6. £1·18 × 3 = £3·54
7. 43 ÷ 6 = $\boxed{7}$ r $\boxed{1}$
8. $\boxed{57}$ − 3 − 4 = 50
9. 146 + 16 = 162
10. (81 ÷ 9) + 15 = 24
11. 0·2 × 100 = 20
12. $\boxed{4003}$, 3994, 3985, 3976
13. 37p + 93p = £1·30
14. 7 + 3 + 65 + 8 = 83
15. 78 $\boxed{\div}$ 6 = 13

Copy and fill in the missing numbers.

```
  4 [3] 2 1
+ 5 6 [9] 9
-----------
  1 0 0 2 0
```

D

1. Write three hundred and fifty thousand and eleven as a number.   350 011
2. (5 × 6) ÷ 2 = 15
3. Imagine a 0 to 99 number square. Which numbers are diagonally below 81?
   90 and 92
4. Write the next multiple of 4:
   84, 88, 92, $\boxed{96}$
5. Two numbers multiplied together make 130. If one of them is 5, what is the other?   26
6. What is the difference between fifty-four and thirty-five?   nineteen
7. Estimate 281 − 111 to the nearest ten.   170
8. $\frac{2}{7}$ of 28 = 8
9. It takes 55 minutes to travel from Brighton to London Victoria, and a further 28 minutes to Willesden Green. How long is the whole journey?   1 h 23 min
10. Which is larger, $\frac{1}{5}$ or 50%?   50%
11. 7 kg + 320 g + 68 g = $\boxed{7388}$ g
12. A florist divides 60 flowers into 4 bouquets of the same size. How many flowers are in each?   15
13. On Tuesday $\frac{1}{5}$ of our class was absent. Write those who were here as a fraction. $\frac{4}{5}$
14. If the shaded area is 8cm², what is the total area of this shape? $\boxed{12}$ cm²
15. Start: 17:35   Finish: (clock) p.m.
    How much time has passed?   2 h 20 min

Exercise 27

A

1. £5·73 + £2·15 = £7·88
2. 78 + 17 = 95
3. [16] ÷ 4 = 4
4. 21 + [21] = 42
5. [69] − 43 = 26
6. 7 × [7] = 49
7. [87] − 9 = 78
8. [4339], 4340, 4341, 4342
9. 0·3 × 100 = 30
10. 73 + 8 − 1 = 80
11. (4 × 10) + 13 = 53
12. 123 − 12 = 111
13. 221 × 4 = 884
14. −6   2   10   [18]
15. [6003], 6012, 6021, 6030

Use squared paper to plot the co-ordinates, then connect them in order.

(0,−1), (1,−3) (2,−1) (4,−6) (5,−4) (6,−6) (6,−1) (5,−3) (4,−1) (2,−6) (1,−4) (0,−6) (0,−1)

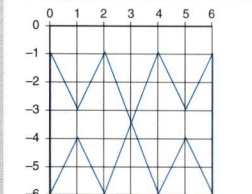

B

1. Round 6403 to the nearest 10.   6400
2. Put these numbers in order, smallest first:
   62 498, 62 894, 63 459, 61 372
   61 372, 62 498, 62 894, 63 459
3. In the number 4382 which digit tell us how many units there are?   2
4. Twenty-two subtract thirteen = 9
5. How many odd numbers are there between 730 and 740?   5
6. [2]5 − 6 = 19
7. 9² + 17 = 98
8. There are 98 children in the infant school. 39 of them have gone on a school trip. How many are left?   59
9. How many is eight times four?   32
10. 15, 21, 36 are multiples of which number?   3
11. Which is larger, $\frac{1}{10}$, 0·25 or 30%?   30%
12. Are these lines parallel?   no 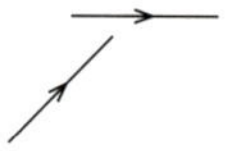
13. Write the co-ordinates.   (3,2) 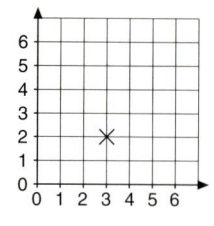
14. What is my change from £2·00 after I have spent £1·40 and 42p?   18p
15. How much time has passed?   4h 35 min

C

1. $\boxed{9} \times 9 = 81$

2. £3·54 − £2·47 = £1·07

3. $14 \div \boxed{7} = 2$

4. $\boxed{34} + 13 = 47$

5. 9321, 9320, $\boxed{9319}$, 9318

6. £1·13 × 2 = £2·26

7. $42 \div 5 = \boxed{8}$ r $\boxed{2}$

8. $\boxed{50} - 3 - 6 = 41$

9. 358 + 13 = 371

10. (56 ÷ 7) + 17 = 25

11. 0·5 × 80 = 40

12. 1002, $\boxed{996}$, 990, 984

13. 67p + 74p = £1·41

14. 28 + 4 + 8 + 8 = 48

15. $7 \boxed{\times} 13 = 91$

Can you make 160 using any of the four operations and some or all of these numbers?

    7   4
         39
    83
         278

D

1. Write nine hundred and eighty thousand, two hundred and twenty-four as a number.   980 224

2. (6 × 6) ÷ 12 = 3

3. Imagine a 0 to 99 number square. Which numbers are diagonally to the left of 31?   20 and 40

4. Write the next multiple of 7: 196, 203, 210, $\boxed{217}$

5. Two numbers multiplied together make 196. If one of them is 7, what is the other?   28

6. What is the difference between seventy-eight and fifty-nine?   nineteen

7. Estimate 891 − 477 to the nearest ten.   410

8. $\frac{3}{4}$ of 36 = 27

9. Mum bought a plant for £2·50 and a basket for £3·75. How much money did she spend?   £6·25

10. Which is larger, $\frac{3}{4}$ or 50%? $\frac{3}{4}$

11. 9 litres + 432 ml + 40 ml = $\boxed{9472}$ ml

12. There are 52 cards in a pack of playing cards. How many of each suit are there?   13

13. Tim gave away 0·75 of his football card collection. Write what was left as a fraction. $\frac{1}{4}$

14. If each square represents 1cm² , what is the area of this shape? $\boxed{21}$ cm²

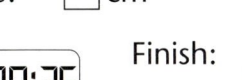

15. Start: 20:25   Finish: (clock) a.m.
    How much time has passed?   2h 30 min or $2\frac{1}{2}$ hours

Exercise 28

A

1. £4·67 + £3·18 = £7·85
2. 86 + 19 = 105
3. 48 ÷ [6] = 8
4. [54] + 32 = 86
5. 59 − 26 = 33
6. [5] × 9 = 45
7. 72 − [5] = 67
8. [6204], 6205, 6206, 6207
9. 25% of 100 = 25
10. 53 − 8 + 6 = 51
11. (3 × 7) + 17 = 38
12. 857 − 26 = 831
13. 213 × 3 = 639
14. [−5] −1 3 7
15. 6217, 6223, 6229, [6235]

Copy and complete.

−	16	29	21	25
65	49	36	44	40
73	57	44	52	48
49	33	20	28	24
35	19	6	14	10

B

1. Round 9511 to the nearest 10. 9510
2. Put these numbers in order, smallest first: 76 419, 74 619, 79 416, 76 918
   74 619, 76 419, 76 918, 79 416
3. In the number 8425, which digit tells us how many 1000s there are? 8
4. Ninety-two subtract seventy-three = nineteen
5. How many even numbers are there between 927 and 945? 9
6. [8]2 − 4 = 78
7. 10^2 − 15 = 85
8. To make a cake you need 95 g of flour. You have put 45 g into the bowl. How much more must you add? 50 g
9. Glasses come in boxes of 6. How many glasses do I get if I buy 6 boxes? 36
10. 36, 54, 18 are multiples of which number? 9
11. Which is larger, $\frac{3}{4}$ or $\frac{2}{3}$? $\frac{3}{4}$
12. Are these lines parallel? yes
13. Write the co-ordinates. (2,5)
14. What is my change from £2·00 when I have spent £1·10 and 39p? 51p
15. How much time has passed? 3h 45 min or $3\frac{3}{4}$ hours

C

1. $\boxed{4} \times 8 = 32$
2. £7·46 − £5·35 = £2·11
3. $60 \div \boxed{6} = 10$
4. $\boxed{23} + 16 = 39$
5. 6101, 6100, $\boxed{6099}$, 6098
6. £1·14 × 6 = £6·84
7. $52 \div 8 = \boxed{6}$ r $\boxed{4}$
8. $\boxed{101} - 8 - 2 = 91$
9. 734 + 17 = 751
10. (21 ÷ 3) + 16 = 23
11. 0·25 × 100 = 25
12. 7011, 7003, $\boxed{6995}$, 6987
13. 43p + 66p = £1·09
14. 4 + 2 + 41 + 9 = 56
15. $144 \boxed{\div} 12 = 12$

How many ways can you make $5\frac{2}{5}$? Here is one example.

$7 - 1\frac{3}{5} = 5\frac{2}{5}$

D

1. Write seven hundred and four thousand, nine hundred and twenty as a number. 704 920
2. (12 × 2) ÷ 8 = 3
3. Imagine a 0 to 99 number square. Which numbers are diagonally to the right of 88? 79 and 99
4. Write the next multiple of 6: 228, 234, 240, $\boxed{246}$
5. Two numbers multiplied together make 112. If one of them is 4, what is the other? 28
6. What is the difference between eighty-six and forty-eight? eighteen
7. Estimate 498 − 268 to the nearest ten. 230
8. $\frac{4}{5}$ of 45 = 36
9. Miller is 38 years old. How old will he be in 35 years time? 73
10. Which is larger, 0·5 or 20%? 0·5
11. 370 ml + 2 litres + 410 ml = $\boxed{2780}$ ml
12. Each night Jena reads the same number of pages. After a week she has read 63 pages. How many pages does she read each night? 9
13. Our class is going to the zoo. We have travelled 25% of the journey. Write what fraction is left. $\frac{3}{4}$
14. If each square represents 1cm², what is the area of this shape? $10\frac{1}{2}$ or 10·5 cm²
15. Start: 02:50   Finish: (clock) a.m.
    How much time has passed? 7 h 20 min

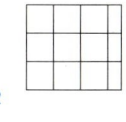

Exercise 29

A

1. £2·23 + £2·19 = £4·42
2. 75 + 28 = 103
3. [18] ÷ 3 = 6
4. 70 + [22] = 92
5. [73] − 32 = 41
6. [11] × 5 = 55
7. 53 − [7] = 46
8. 8498, 8499, [8500], 8501
9. 50% of 100 = 50
10. 88 + 7 − 6 = 89
11. (6 × 2) + 14 = 26
12. 498 − 35 = 463
13. 342 × 2 = 684
14. −10 −4 [2] 8
15. [9496], 9503, 9510, 9517

Copy and complete
the Decimal Function Machine
add 0·9

in	out
3·451	4·351
1·258	2·158
6·237	7·137
3·37	4·27
5·614	6·514
8·532	9·432
6·224	7·124
8·61	9·51
8·407	9·307

B

1. Round 4369 to the nearest 10.   4370
2. Put these numbers in order, smallest first:
93 504, 90 534, 93 054, 93 540
90 534, 93 054, 93 504, 93 540
3. In the number 9438, which digit tells us how many units there are?   8
4. Forty-one subtract thirty-six = five
5. How many odd numbers are there between 294 and 306?   6
6. [5]4 − 7 = 47
7. 5^2 − 12 = 13
8. Faisal had 36 children at his party. If 19 were boys, how many were girls?   17
9. Chairs have 4 legs. If there are 8 chairs around a table, how many legs are there?   32
10. 24, 40, 64 are multiples of which number?   8
11. Which is larger, $\frac{3}{4}$ $\frac{2}{5}$ or $\frac{1}{3}$? $\frac{3}{4}$
12. Are these lines parallel?   no
13. Write the co-ordinates.   (3,4)
14. What is my change from £2·00 after I have spent £1·40 and 42p?   18p
15. How much time has passed?   1h 10 min

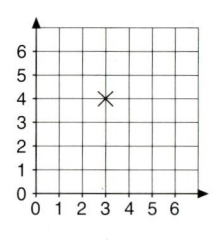

C

1. $\boxed{8} \times 6 = 48$

2. £3·26 − £1·19 = £2·07

3. 36 ÷ $\boxed{4}$ = 9

4. $\boxed{14}$ + 14 = 28

5. 4302, 4301, 4300, $\boxed{4299}$

6. £1·18 × 4 = £4·72

7. 37 ÷ 7 = $\boxed{5}$ r $\boxed{2}$

8. $\boxed{80}$ − 4 − 7 = 69

9. 554 + 28 = 582

10. (20 ÷ 2) + 14 = 24

11. 0·5 × 40 = 20

12. 6121, 6113, 6105, $\boxed{6097}$

13. 78p + 43p = £1·21

14. 3 + 27 + 4 + 6 = 40

15. 57 $\boxed{-}$ 29 = 28

★ Copy and fill in the missing numbers.

```
  3 4 6
− 1 8 8
-------
  1 5 8
```

D

1. Write four hundred and sixty thousand, three hundred and one as a number.
460 301

2. (7 × 4) ÷ 14 = 2

3. Imagine a 0 to 99 number square. Which numbers are diagonally to the left of 11?
0 and 20

4. Write the next multiple of 9:
621, 630, 639, $\boxed{648}$

5. Two numbers multiplied together make 144. If one of them is 6, what is the other? 24

6. What is the difference between fifty-five and twenty-six? 29

7. Estimate 728 − 341 to the nearest ten.
390

8. $\frac{4}{7}$ of 42 = 24

9. My car shows a mileage of 2357 miles. If I drive a further 36 miles, what will my mileage be then? 2393

10. Which is larger, 33% or $\frac{1}{5}$? 33%

11. 230 g + 5 kg + 620 g = $\boxed{5850}$ g

12. There are 100 families living in 4 blocks of flats.
How many families are in each block? 25

13. Sylvia has read $\frac{3}{4}$ of a book.
What fraction is left? $\frac{1}{4}$

14. If each square represents 1 cm², what is the area of this shape? 7·5 or $7\frac{1}{2}$ cm

15. Start: (clock showing) Finish: 09:15 a.m.

How much time has passed? 6 h 30 min

Exercise 30

A

1. £5·67 + £3·28 = £8·95
2. 43 + 39 = 82
3. 72 ÷ 9 = 8
4. 22 + 41 = 63
5. 67 − 46 = 21
6. 12 × 4 = 48
7. 65 − 6 = 59
8. 5493, 5494, 5495, 5496
9. $\frac{1}{4}$ of 200 = 50
10. 64 − 7 + 8 = 65
11. (5 × 4) + 16 = 36
12. 764 − 22 = 742
13. 211 × 4 = 844
14. −2, 0, 2, 4
15. 7205, 7210, 7215, 7220

Use squared paper to plot the co-ordinates, then connect them in order.

(−5,2) (−2,6) (−3,1) (−4,6) (−2,4) (−5,2)

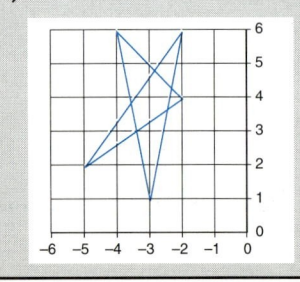

B

1. Round 5426 to the nearest 10. 5430
2. Put these numbers in order, smallest first:
   46 315, 46 314, 46 415, 46 414
   46 314, 46 315, 46 414, 46 415
3. In the number 7219, which digit tell us how many 10s there are? 1
4. Fifty-three subtract twenty-seven = twenty-six
5. How many even numbers are there between 593 and 607? 7
6. 9 3 − 8 = 85
7. 6² + 14 = 50
8. The prices in a shop are reduced by 15p. How much does a chocolate bar that was 99p now cost? 84p
9. What is the product of three and seven?
   twenty-one
10. 21, 42, 56 are multiples of which number? 7
11. Which is larger, $\frac{2}{3}$ $\frac{3}{4}$ or $\frac{2}{5}$? $\frac{3}{4}$
12. Draw a set of parallel lines. answers will vary
13. Write the co-ordinates.
    (1,2) 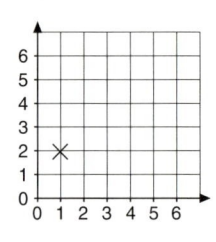
14. What is my change from £2·00 after I have spent £1·60 and 39p? 1p
15. How much time has passed?
    2h 15 min or $2\frac{1}{4}$ hours

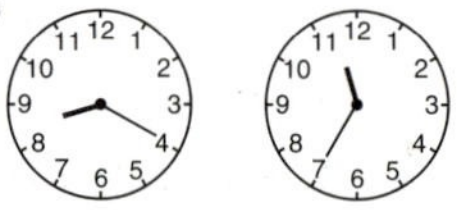

C

1. $\boxed{8} \times 9 = 72$
2. £5·82 − £3·75 = £2·07
3. 28 ÷ $\boxed{7}$ = 4
4. $\boxed{49}$ + 12 = 61
5. $\boxed{7000}$, 6999, 6998, 6997
6. £1·11 × 3 = £3·33
7. 68 ÷ 9 = $\boxed{7}$ r $\boxed{5}$
8. $\boxed{105}$ − 7 − 5 = 93
9. 878 + 16 = 894
10. (16 ÷ 4) + 11 = 15
11. 0·25 × 400 = 100
12. 5034, 5027, 5020, $\boxed{5013}$
13. 25p + 99p = £1·24
14. 8 + 9 + 43 + 7 = 67
15. 57 $\boxed{+}$ 39 = 96

Can you make 681 using any of the four operations and some or all of these numbers?

9
519
2
72
35

D

1. Write five hundred thousand two hundred and six as a number. 500 206
2. (4 × 9) ÷ 3 = 12
3. Imagine a 0 to 99 number square. Which numbers are diagonally to the right of 17? 8 and 28
4. Write the next multiple of 3: 288, 291, 294, $\boxed{297}$
5. Two numbers multiplied together make 176. If one of them is 8, what is the other? 22
6. What is the difference between sixty-three and thirty-four? twenty-nine
7. Estimate 531 − 297 to the nearest ten. 230
8. $\frac{5}{6}$ of 54 = 45
9. The price of a 37p-packet of crisps goes up by 14p. What is the new price? 51p
10. Which is larger, 0·25 or $\frac{1}{3}$? $\frac{1}{3}$
11. 2 km + 300 m + 16 m = $\boxed{2316}$ m
12. If a jug holds 75 ml of juice, how many 25 ml glasses can you fill? 3
13. If $\frac{1}{4}$ of our school bring packed lunches, what fraction have school dinners? $\frac{3}{4}$
14. If each square represents 1 cm², what is the area of this shape? $8\frac{1}{4}$ or 8·25 cm²
15. Start: 19:45 Finish: a.m.
    How much time has passed? 6h 45 min

Heinemann Educational Publishers
Halley Court, Jordan Hill, Oxford OX2 8EJ
a division of Reed Educational & Professional
Publishing Ltd

Oxford Melbourne Auckland
Florence Prague Madrid Athens
Singapore Tokyo Sao Paulo
Chicago Portsmouth NH (USA) Mexico City
Ibadan Gaborone Johannesburg
Kampala Nairobi Kuala Lumpur

© Peter Clarke and Christina Rossiter 1997

All rights reserved. No part of this publication may be reproduced, stored in a retrieval system, or transmitted in any form or by any means, electronic, mechanical, photocopying, recording, or otherwise without either the prior written permission of the Publishers or a licence permitting restricted copying in the United Kingdom issued by the Copyright Licensing Agency Ltd, 90 Tottenham Court Road, London W1P 3HE.

First published 1997

00 99 98 97
10 9 8 7 6 5 4 3 2

ISBN 0435 02431 0
pack of 8 pupil books: 0435 02418 3

Designed by Artistix
Typeset and illustrated by TechType, Abingdon, Oxon.
Cover design by Peter Campbell
Printed and bound by Scotprint